same-sex

marriage in the united states

POST–2004 ELECTION EDITION

same-sex
marriage in the united states

FOCUS

ON THE FACTS

SEAN CAHILL, PH.D.

LEXINGTON BOOKS
Lanham • Boulder • New York • Toronto • Oxford

LEXINGTON BOOKS

Published in the United States of America
by Lexington Books
An imprint of The Rowman & Littlefield Publishing Group, Inc.
4501 Forbes Boulevard, Suite 200, Lanham, Maryland 20706

PO Box 317
Oxford
OX2 9RU, UK

British Library Cataloguing in Publication Information Available

Library of Congress Cataloging-in-Publication Data
Cahill, Sean (Sean Robert)
    Same-sex marriage in the United States : focus on the facts, post–2004 election edition /
Sean Cahill.
       p. cm.
    Includes bibliographical references and index.
    ISBN 0-7391-0881-6 (hardcover : alk. paper) — ISBN 0-7391-0882-4 (pbk. : alk.
paper)
    1. Same-sex marriage—United States.   2. Same-sex marriage—Law and legislation—
United States.   3. Same-sex marriage—Political aspects—United States.
4. Homophobia—United States.   5. Gay rights—United States.   I. Title.

HQ1034.U5C34 2004
306.84'8'0973—dc22   2004013082

Printed in the United States of America

∞™ The paper used in this publication meets the minimum requirements of American
National Standard for Information Sciences—Permanence of Paper for Printed Library
Materials, ANSI/NISO Z39.48-1992.

Contents

Preface

Since the middle of 2003, Americans have been inundated with images of and claims about same-sex marriage. For many, the marriage issue is something onto which they project their deepest anxieties and hopes: same-sex marriage is a nefarious assault on a pillar of Western civilization; same-sex marriage is a sellout of a once liberationist movement; same-sex marriage is the latest front in the struggle for a more equitable society. During the course of this debate, many claims have been made that are untrue. Terms such as *civil union, domestic partnership,* and *civil marriage*—the vocabulary of the debate—appear frequently in the media and confuse even gay and lesbian couples. The state of the law in this area is unclear, as same-sex couples have married in several cities and counties whose state governments have not yet legalized gay marriage. And many elected officials have taken confusing and seemingly contradictory positions, opposing gay marriage but at the same time opposing efforts to write a ban into the U.S. Constitution. This book sorts through this confusion, presenting the facts about gay couple families, the facts about the pro- and anti-gay marriage movements, and how this issue has played out in American politics, particularly in recent presidential elections. Everything in this book is true, and as many claims are cited as possible.

THE STRUCTURE OF THIS BOOK

Chapter 1 lays out the current terrain. It reviews the three key court decisions in 2003 that sparked the current debate: the Ontario marriage ruling, the U.S. Supreme Court's *Lawrence v. Texas* decision, and the Massachusetts marriage ruling. It summarizes previous efforts to legally restrict same-sex marriage starting in the mid-1990s, and fits current attempts to ban gay marriage into this recent historical context. Chapter 1 also describes the distinction between religious marriage and civil marriage, as well as the difference between marriage and civil unions. Only equal access to the institution of marriage offers same-sex couples full and complete equality.

Chapter 2 examines the worldview of the national and local anti-gay groups leading the charge against same-sex marriage. Most of these groups are religion-based. Although these groups have found a home in the Republican Party and the Bush Administration and are frequently quoted alongside gay people and pro-gay elected officials, they promote a highly reactionary political agenda. Many oppose any form of legal equality for gay people and oppose nondiscrimination policies. Many also oppose affirmative action, reproductive choice, teaching evolution, sex education, women in combat, and no-fault divorce. Anti-gay groups greatly out-spend gay advocacy groups. And they regularly rely on myths and false statements about gay people, for example, that there is an intrinsic link between pedophilia and homosexuality, and that the legalization of gay marriage could mean that anti-gay parents could be sent to jail and lose custody of their children. They portray gay parents as a threat to their own children. In addition to presenting a few of the most egregious claims, I present social science research that refutes them.

Such campaigns inevitably have a negative effect on gay people, even if anti-gay forces lose the fight to pass an anti-gay law or to prevent passage of a pro-gay law. New York City's Gay and Lesbian Anti-Violence Project has documented a 53% increase in anti-gay violence and harassment in the second half of 2003 compared to the last six months of 2002.[1] This period corresponds to the anti-gay movement's orchestrated campaign against the pro-gay court rulings of June 2003.[2]

Chapter 3 provides a brief overview of the myriad family policy issues affecting gay and lesbian people and same-sex couples, which include bisexual individuals as well. These issues include parenting—which is more prevalent among gay and lesbian couples than many may think. Many lesbian couples in particular include a biological mother and a nonbiological mother. While 23 states have allowed nonbiological mothers to adopt through a process known as second-parent adoption, 27 states do not recognize such adoptions. This means that many nonbiological lesbian mothers who have raised their children since birth are legally strangers to their own children. Six states limit or ban gay people or same-sex couples from adopting or serving as foster parents.

Seniors who are gay or lesbian also face discrimination and sometimes even abuse and neglect in long-term care settings. Critical policies like Social Security, pensions, and Medicaid do not treat same-sex partners equally, restricting elders' options and creating insecurity in old age, when many elders are on a limited income. Similarly, many health policies treat same-sex couples unfairly. For example, the federal Family and Medical Leave Act does not allow gay partners to take unpaid leave from work to care for their loved ones. Domestic partner health insurance, if it is offered, is taxed as income, while spousal health benefits are tax-exempt. Gay couples pay more in taxes, but they are not eligible for 1,138 federal programs that are contingent upon marital status. Finally, anti-gay and religious discrimination in social services, which have already occurred under the faith-based initiative, is also an impending threat.

Chapter 4 examines how anti-gay political groups became an integral part of the Republican coalition. I trace the emergence of anti-gay activism as a central focus of the religious right to the first anti-gay ballot measures of the 1970s and the first anti-gay advertisements in a presidential campaign—those used successfully by the Reagan campaign in 1980. I examine the anti-gay movement's exploitation of the AIDS crisis to mobilize animosity toward gay people and the upsurge in activity in the late 1980s and early 1990s under the banner "No Special Rights." This culminated in the prominent role anti-gay speakers played at the 1992 Republican Convention.

I also trace the emergence of a movement for gay equality and its close relationship with the Democratic Party, dating back as far as 1972. Although nationally the Democrats held gay supporters at arm's length throughout the 1980s, Bill Clinton was the first presidential candidate to articulate a vision of America that included gay men and lesbians. Anti-gay groups scored two major victories in the 1990s—quashing efforts to lift the military ban on openly gay service members in 1993 and banning federal recognition of same-sex marriage in 1996. Despite a dramatic growth in nondiscrimination laws, public opinion support for gay equality, and the emergence of a sizable gay voting bloc, anti-gay activists succeeded in preventing sex education and tolerance education. Thirty-nine states have banned same-sex marriage, and legislatures in two dozen states as well as Congress are considering constitutional amendments to further define marriage as an exclusively heterosexual institution. Many of these would also ban more limited forms of family recognition, such as partner health insurance.

Chapter 4 concludes with a look at the general opposition of the Bush–Cheney Administration to legal equality for gay people, and at the way gay issues played out in the 2004 presidential campaign and election. While Bush puts forth a "compassionate conservative" image, he opposes most forms of legal equality for gay people. Bush's focus on gay marriage diverted attention from the failures of his administration at home and abroad. Emerging from the most pro-gay field of presidential candidates yet, Senator John Kerry supports legal equality for gay people in most areas except marriage. He took an inconsistent position—opposing the Federal Marriage

Amendment while supporting similar measures in Massachusetts and Missouri. The issue clearly played a role in the 2004 election.

Chapter 5 profiles two lesbian and gay couples whose inability to marry cost them basic benefits and services following the tragic death of their life partners. It then describes the anti-gay movement's lobbying campaign against providing benefits or services to the surviving gay partners of the victims of the 9/11 terrorist attacks. Trends in public opinion on same-sex partner recognition, including marriage, are described, and the American debate over marriage equality is fit into a broader international context in which countries around the world are ahead of the United States in terms of basic rights accorded gay partners of their citizens.

As this updated edition goes to press in December 2004, thousands of same-sex couples have been married in Massachusetts. They are married according to the laws of the Commonwealth of Massachusetts, their marriages are recognized by the courts, and they enjoy the rights and privileges the state confers on all married couples. However, unlike most married couples in the United States, these newlyweds may be "de-married," their rights and privileges removed. On March 29, 2004, the Massachusetts legislature, by a narrow margin, voted for a constitutional amendment defining marriage as a union between only one man and one woman. If the legislature again passes the amendment in the next session (2005–2006), it will appear on the ballot in November 2006. If the amendment is ratified by a majority of voters, Massachusetts could become the first state to take away the rights of same-sex married couples.

The U.S. Senate voted on and rejected the Federal Marriage Amendment just before the Democratic Convention in July 2004. A week later, the U.S. House of Representatives approved a bill that would strip federal courts of jurisdiction over cases involving same-sex marriage. This court-stripping bill undermines the principle of judicial review established by *Marbury v. Madison* in 1803. In 2004, 13 states voted on amendments that make gay marriage illegal and, in 9 of the 13, limit other forms of partner recognition for gay and straight unmarried couples as well. In November 2004, 21 million Americans voted on gay marriage, even though most voters ranked gay marriage among the least of this nation's problems. The political focus on same-sex marriage detracted attention from the volatile and dangerous situation in Iraq, the record job losses, the burgeoning federal budget deficit, and many other areas in urgent need of aid. It is to show—in plain language, supported by the facts—how we have come to this point, to offer a corrective to the imbalance, and to provide a voice of reason in a heated debate that I offer this book.

Acknowledgments

I dedicate this book to my father and mother. Thanks, for research assistance: Micah Carvalho, Jason Cianciotto, Rod Colvin, Alain Dang, Dulani, Mitra Ellen, Paula Ettelbrick, Sarah Holmes, Juan Hernandez, Rachel Hill, Mandy Hu, Pavita Krishnaswamy, Ruth McFarlane, Kristen Nosek, Adam Pedersen-Doherty, Randy Reyes, Frank Roberts, Bernard Schlotfeldt, Ken South, Dean Spade, Sarah Tobias, Marie Varghese, and Dawn Walsh. Thanks to the Task Force staff, board, and funders; Serena Leigh Krombach, Ginger Strader, and Samuel Buggeln for editing/design; Ivan Cheung and Kirsten Barrett, maps. For their inspirational research: Urvashi Vaid, Bob Bailey, Juan Battle, Cathy Cohen, Chip Berlet, Jean Hardisty, Alan Yang, Lee Badgett, Glenn Magpantay, Darren Rosenblum, Judith Bradford, Charlotte Patterson, Ken Sherrill, Rafael Diaz, George Cheung, Steve Haeberle, Marjorie Cantor, Andrew Shippy, Randy Sell, John D'Emilio, Gary Gates, Eric Rofes, and Terence Dougherty. For their vision: Sue Hyde, Arline Isaacson, Josh Friedes, Mary Bonauto, Jason Riggs, Arthur Lipkin, Marc Solomon, Valerie Fein-Zachary, Jeremy Pittman, Mary Breslauer, Gary Daffin, Marty Rouse, Evan Wolfson, Kevin Cathcart, Kate Kendall, Matt Coles, Mandy Carter, Alexander Robinson, Patrick Guerriero, Matt Foreman, Kerry Lobel, Lorri Jean, Darrel Cummings, Clarence Patton, Tim McFeeley, Tim Davis, Barbara Hoffman; Reps. Byron Rushing, Liz Malia, Alice Wolf, Jay Kaufman, Paul Demakis, Marie St. Fleur, Gloria Fox, Ruth Balser, Sal DiMasi, Martin Walsh, Mary Grant, Barbara L'Italien, Ted Speliotis; Sens. Dianne Wilkerson, Jarrett Barrios, Tom Birmingham, Brian Joyce, Steve Tolman, Patricia Haddad; Mayors Thomas Menino and David Cohen, Charlotte Richie, Maureen Feeney, Rosaria Salerno, Marjorie Claprood, my family.

Fast Facts

1

A Fierce Debate

LANDMARK DECISIONS

In 2003, the debate over whether or not to allow same-sex couples access to the institution of civil marriage emerged as a major political issue in the United States. This resulted from three landmark court decisions:

1. June 10, 2003: Ontario's high court rules that same-sex couples should have the right to marry under the nation's charter of rights.[1]

On June 10, 2003, an Ontario appeals court ruled that seven same-sex couples had the right to marry. The three-judge panel ruled unanimously that Canada's Charter of Rights and Freedoms—"Canada's version of the Bill of Rights," according to the *New York Times*[2]—mandated equal access to civil marriage for gay and lesbian couples. "Same-sex couples are capable of forming long, lasting, loving and intimate relationships," the court ruled, and extending the right to marry to gay couples would cause no harm to the rest of the community.[3] Canada's Prime Minister Jean Chretien quickly endorsed the ruling and introduced a bill into Parliament to nationalize its impact.[4]

June 10, 2003: Ontario's high court rules that same-sex couples should have the right to marry under the nation's charter of rights.

One month later, British Columbia's appeals court issued a similar ruling.[5] Same-sex couples were now getting married in two of Canada's provinces comprising half the country's population. Among those flocking to Toronto and Vancouver to wed were hundreds of American gay couples. In March 2004, Quebec followed suit,[6] meaning that three-quarters of Canadians now live in a province that allows gay marriage.

June 26, 2003: The U.S. Supreme Court rules that anti-gay sodomy laws violate the U.S. Constitution's right to privacy.

2. June 26, 2003: The U.S. Supreme Court rules that anti-gay sodomy laws violate the U.S. Constitution's right to privacy.[7]

In June 2003, the U.S. Supreme Court struck down laws in 13 states banning private, consensual sexual intimacy. Widely known as "sodomy laws," nine of these laws banned certain practices regardless of whether the couple engaging in them was heterosexual or homosexual. The other four states' laws banned certain sexual practices only for homosexual couples. The court's 6-3 ruling that such laws violated the Constitution's privacy provision did not directly address the issue of state recognition of same-sex marriages. However, there was much language in the majority decision that both gay rights proponents and opponents said could be used to promote marriage equality. Justice Anthony Kennedy, writing for the majority, ruled that the state cannot single out gay people for harassment and discriminatory treatment simply because of "moral disapproval" of homosexuality.[8] Kennedy wrote of "respect" for gay couples and warned that "the state cannot demean their existence." The court also described gay relationships as a "personal bond" involving much more than just sex.[9] Kennedy said reducing gay couples to "sex partners," as anti-gay organizations often do, is offensive in the same way that describing a husband and wife as nothing more than sex partners would be offensive. However, apparently cognizant of the marriage challenges pending in New Jersey and Massachusetts, and that some might interpret the *Lawrence* ruling as supporting marriage equality for gay couples, Kennedy made a point of noting that the case against the Texas sodomy law "does not involve whether the government must give formal recognition to any relationship homosexual persons seek to enter." In her concurrence, Justice Sandra Day O'Connor said that the "traditional institution of marriage" was not at issue.[10]

Despite these majority caveats, Justice Antonin Scalia argued just the opposite in his dissent, in which he was joined by Chief Justice William Rehnquist: "Today's opinion dismantles the structure of constitutional law that has permitted a distinction to be made between heterosexual and homosexual unions, insofar as formal recognition in marriage is concerned."[11] Anti-gay activists and politicians quickly and vocally agreed, to the point that the decision repealing archaic, often colonial-era sodomy laws in 13 states became increasingly portrayed in the mainstream media as a precursor to legalization of gay marriage. Rev. Jerry Falwell warned that "it's a capitulation to the gay and lesbian agenda whose ultimate goal is the legalization of same-sex marriages."[12] Republican Senator Rick Santorum of Pennsylvania warned that "the greatest near-term consequence of the *Lawrence v. Texas* anti-sodomy ruling could be the legalization of homosexual marriage."[13] Gay rights activists found themselves in the unusual position of agreeing with Falwell, Scalia, and Santorum: "I think it's inevitable now," said the Lambda Legal Defense and Education Fund's Patricia Logue, co-counsel in the *Lawrence* case, of legalized same-sex marriage. "In what time frame, we don't know."[14] *Lawrence* lead attorney Ruth Harlow, also with Lambda, said, "The ruling makes it much harder for society to continue banning gay marriages."[15]

November 18, 2003: The Massachusetts Supreme Judicial Court rules that denying marriage to same-sex couples violates that state's constitutional guarantees of equal protection and due process.

3. November 18, 2003: The Massachusetts Supreme Judicial Court rules that denying marriage to same-sex couples violates that state's constitutional guarantees of equal protection and due process.[16]

On November 18, 2003, the Massachusetts Supreme Judicial Court declared that marriage is a civil right and that gays and lesbians have a constitutional right, under the due process and equal protection provisions of the Massachusetts Constitution, to marry the person of their choice: "Limiting the protections, benefits, and obligations of civil marriage to opposite-sex couples violates the basic premises of individual liberty and equality under law protected by the Massachusetts Constitution."[17]

"We construe civil marriage to mean the voluntary union of two persons as spouses, to the exclusion of all others," the majority wrote. "This reformulation redresses the plaintiffs' constitutional injury, and furthers the aim of marriage to promote stable, exclusive relationships." The court rejected claims by some opponents of same-sex marriage that allowing gay and lesbian couples to marry would undermine the institution of marriage: "Extending civil marriage to same-sex couples reinforces the importance of marriage to individuals and communities. That same-sex couples are willing to embrace marriage's solemn obligations of exclusivity, mutual support, and commitment to one another is a testament to the enduring place of marriage in our laws and in the human spirit."

In its decision, the court noted the critical distinction between civil and religious marriage, that "civil unions" for gay couples were a separate and unequal, unsatisfactory option, and that children as well as their gay or lesbian parents suffered from the inability to marry.

In the wake of the Massachusetts high court ruling in late 2003, Massachusetts state legislators asked whether civil unions, which afford nearly all the benefits of marriage at the level of state policy (but none of the 1,138 federal benefits), would suffice to meet the court's ruling. In February 2004, the court answered that civil unions would not suffice, as they would continue "to relegate same-sex couples to . . . second-class status." The court noted that "the history of our nation has demonstrated that separate is seldom, if ever, equal."[18] This second ruling reaffirmed the right of same-sex couples to marry.

On November 29, 2004, the United States Supreme Court declined to overturn the Massachusetts Supreme Judicial Court's ruling in *Goodridge*. The Catholic Action League of Massachusetts had asked for the ruling to be overturned on the grounds that the justices had exceeded their authority and usurped the power of the Massachusetts legislature. The U.S. Supreme Court rejected this claim; for now, at least, the Massachusetts court's action in *Goodridge* stands.

LEGISLATIVE EFFORTS TO RESTRICT SAME-SEX MARRIAGE

These rulings took place in a legislative climate that had recently become more restrictive, on both the federal and state levels, regarding a couple's right to marry.

The Federal Defense of Marriage Act

In 1993, the Hawaii Supreme Court launched an important and ongoing international debate when it ruled that it was impermissible gender discrimination under the state constitution to deny three lesbian and gay couples the right to obtain a marriage license.[19] This decision stated that Hawaii could only deny the marriage licenses if it could indicate a compelling reason to do so. In 1996, a Hawaii trial court found that the state had failed to justify its denial with a compelling reason and so the couples did have the right to marry under civil law.

In reaction to these developments, in 1996 Congress passed the Defense of Marriage Act (DOMA), which

The 1996 Defense of Marriage Act defines marriage in federal law as a "legal union between one man and one woman," thereby restricting federal benefits to heterosexual couples.

defined marriage in federal law as a "legal union between one man and one woman," thereby restricting federal benefits, such as Social Security survivor benefits, to heterosexual couples. The bill also told states they did not have to recognize same-sex marriages should another state legalize such marriages.[20] The bill's 22 conservative Republican sponsors titled it the Defense of Marriage Act, implying that the desire of gay and lesbian couples to marry constitutes an aggression against the traditional heterosexual institution of marriage. President Bill Clinton's expression of opposition to lesbian and gay marriage, and his decision to sign DOMA into law in October 1996, prevented gay marriage from becoming a major campaign issue in the 1996 presidential campaign. It did, however, anger and alienate many of Clinton's gay and liberal supporters.

According to DOMA, states do not have to recognize same-sex marriages that may become legal in another state.

During the debate over DOMA, many elected officials and presidential candidates portrayed gay couples seeking to marry as a threat to the family and Western civilization. Conservative politicians and media picked up and echoed these claims. Congressman Steve Largent (R-OK) likened homosexuality to bestiality and pedophilia when he rhetorically asked how one could support same-sex marriages but oppose legalizing polygamous, pedophile, and bestial "relationships": "There is no reason why we cannot just completely erase whatever boundaries that currently exist on the definition of marriage and say it is a free-for-all, anything goes."[21]

DOMA cosponsor Rep. Robert Barr (R-GA), who had himself divorced multiple times, compared same-sex marriage supporters to those whose decadence allegedly destroyed Rome:

> . . . as Rome burned, Nero fiddled, and that is exactly what [opponents of DOMA] would have us do. . . . The very foundations of our society are in danger of being burned. The flames of hedonism, the flames of narcissism, the

flames of self-centered morality are licking at the very foundations of our society: the family unit.[22]

Rep. Charles Canady (R-FL) echoed Barr, stating that what was at stake was "nothing less than our collective moral understanding, as expressed in law, of the essential nature of the family, the fundamental building block of society."[23] The DOMA sponsors and supporters fail to acknowledge that all gay and lesbian people come from families; that many are in long-term, committed relationships; and that many are raising children and/or serving in caretaker roles to elders or adult family members with disabilities.[24]

While many feel the federal Defense of Marriage Act will be struck down as unconstitutional either for violating the full faith and credit clause or because it represents inappropriate federal usurpation of a state role, the Bush–Cheney Administration has cited it in order to prevent a married Canadian gay couple from entering the United States as a married couple. The couple filled out a joint form, but Customs officials insisted they complete two individual forms. Noting that DOMA is the law of the land, Beth Poisson, press attaché at the U.S. Embassy in Ottawa, said "The Customs officers were upholding U.S. law."[25] It is likely that if gay couples married in Canada or Massachusetts attempt to file joint federal taxes or seek equal treatment under Social Security policy, they will be told that DOMA prevents their being treated equally.

It is likely that if gay couples married in Canada or Massachusetts attempt to file joint federal taxes or seek equal treatment under Social Security policy, they will be told that DOMA prevents their being treated equally.

State DOMAs and Super-DOMAs

While combining the very words *gay* and *marriage* would have evoked mostly confused expressions in the early 1990s, by 1996 Republican presidential candidates were taking the "defense of marriage" pledge, and both houses of Congress overwhelmingly approved the Defense of Marriage Act. Public officials at all levels of government were asked their position on gay marriage. Newspapers and

Anti-Gay Marriage Measures in the U.S.
As of November 22, 2004

Source: National Gay & Lesbian Task Force, 2004

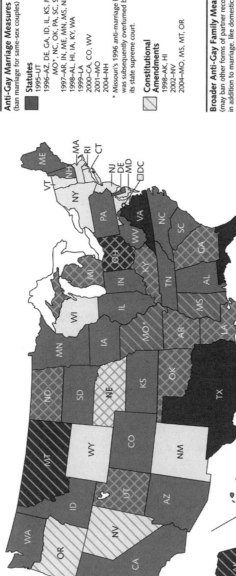

Anti-Gay Marriage Measures
(ban marriage for same-sex couples)

Statutes
1995–UT
1996–AZ, DE, GA, ID, IL, KS, MI, MO*, NC, OK, PA, SC, SD, TN
1997–AR, IN, ME, MN, MS, ND, VA
1998–AL, HI, IA, KY, WA
1999–LA
2000–CA, CO, WV
2001–MO
2004–NH

* Missouri's 1996 anti-marriage law was subsequently overturned by its state supreme court.

Constitutional Amendments
1998–AK, HI
2002–NV
2004–MO, MS, MT, OR

Broader Anti-Gay Family Measures
(may ban other forms of partner recognition in addition to marriage, like domestic partnership and civil unions; some ban these for unmarried opposite-sex couples as well)

Statutes
1997–AK, FL, MT
2003–TX
2004–VA, OH

Constitutional Amendments
2000–NE
2004–LA, AR, GA, KY, MI, ND, OH, OK, UT

In 1996, Congress passed and President Clinton signed into law the "Defense of Marriage Act" (DOMA). It says that no state is required to honor same sex marriages performed in another state. It also seeks to restrict how marriage may be defined or interpreted under federal law to "a legal union between one man and one woman as husband and wife."

Many states have passed both a statute and a constitutional amendment.

talk radio hosts railed against it. Six in 10 Americans polled expressed disapproval of same-sex marriage.[26] A total of 16 states passed anti-gay marriage laws by the end of 1996. Anti-gay marriage bills were defeated or withdrawn in 20 other states. Only 13 states reported no anti-gay marriage legislative activity in 1996.[27] Another 15 states adopted anti-gay marriage laws in 1997 and 1998.[28] As of late 2004, 40 states have such laws. State DOMAs have implications that figure in a variety of cases. For example, in 2002 a Pennsylvania court cited the state's DOMA law to block a second-parent adoption by a same-sex partner. A higher court later reversed the ruling.[29]

A new form of anti-gay marriage legislation is informally referred to as "Super-DOMAs." Building on federal and state Defense of Marriage Acts (DOMAs) that prohibit recognition of the marriages of same-sex couples, Super-DOMAs typically aim to prohibit any kind of recognition of same-sex relationships, including civil unions and domestic partnerships, which offer some of the rights of marriage but not most of the protections, which are federally mandated. These laws or amendments may endanger public-sector employer-provided domestic partner benefits, joint and second-parent adoptions, recognition of same-sex couples' legal contracts, health care decision-making proxies, or indeed any policy currently in effect that recognizes the existence of a same-sex partnership. Nebraska passed a Super-DOMA in 2000,[3] and Ohio and Virginia passed Super-DOMAs in early 2004. Nine of the 13 anti-marriage amendments to state constitutions passed through ballot questions in November 2004 not only ban gay marriage, but also threaten more limited protections for unmarried partners.

The Federal Marriage Amendment

On May 21, 2003, Rep. Marilyn Musgrave (R-CO) introduced H.J. Resolution 56 to amend the U.S. Constitu-

A total of 16 states passed anti-gay marriage laws by the end of 1996. Anti-gay marriage bills were defeated or withdrawn in 20 other states. Only 13 states reported no anti-gay marriage legislative activity in 1996. Another 15 states adopted anti-gay marriage laws in 1997 and 1998. As of late 2004, 40 states have such laws.

tion to define marriage as between a man and a woman, and to prevent legislatures or courts from mandating more limited benefits, such as civil unions or domestic partnerships. The Federal Marriage Amendment failed to win sufficient votes in the U.S. Senate in July 2004 to move forward. Anti-gay activists have vowed to renew their push for its passage in 2005–2006.

The Federal Marriage Amendment (FMA) would short-circuit state efforts to legalize marriage for same-sex couples by banning same-sex marriage and prohibiting courts and legislatures from citing state or federal law, or state or federal constitutions, to mandate more limited forms of recognition, such as hospital visitation rights, domestic partner health benefits, and second-parent adoption. It reads:

> Marriage in the United States shall consist only of the union of a man and a woman. Neither this Constitution nor the Constitution of any State, nor State or Federal law, shall be construed to require that marital status or the legal incidents thereof be conferred upon unmarried couples or groups.[31]

The proposed Constitutional amendment would not only ban civil marriage for same-sex couples. By prohibiting the conferral of "marital status or the legal incidents thereof" on same-sex couples based on an interpretation of the federal Constitution, state constitutions, or state or federal law, the FMA could jeopardize hard-won domestic partner health benefits and registries, offered in nearly a dozen states and hundreds of municipalities, as well as by thousands of private employers. Civil unions, which afford most of the obligations, responsibilities, and recognitions of marriage to Vermont gay couples at the level of state policy, could also be jeopardized.

While anti-gay groups say this would allow legislatures to pass domestic partner and civil union policies, these same groups regularly challenge more limited forms of same-sex partner recognition.[32] The American Center for Law and Justice, founded by the Christian Coalition's Rev. Pat Robertson, filed a lawsuit on behalf of the Catholic Action League of Massachusetts to strike down Boston's municipal domestic partnership policy in 1998–1999.[33] The Center for Marriage Law and the Alliance Defense Fund filed a similar lawsuit against domestic partnership benefits in Portland, Maine.[34] The proposed Federal Marriage Amendment could embolden such challenges and could deter state and local governments from offering domestic partner health insurance to their employees or registries for resident gay couples.

In March 2004, the FMA's lead sponsors amended the proposal's language slightly, removing the phrase "nor State or Federal law" from the second sentence. It now reads:

> Marriage in the United States shall consist only of the union of a man and a woman. Neither this Constitution [n]or the Constitution of any State shall be construed to require that marital status or the legal incidents thereof be conferred upon unmarried couples or groups.[35]

While this change might allow a court to interpret a state nondiscrimination law to require marriage equality, it would still undercut the state constitutional basis for Vermont's 1999 high court ruling that led to civil unions, or for Massachusetts' high court ruling in favor of marriage rights for same-sex couples. Any future rulings in support of protections for gay couples, even short of marriage, based on the equality provisions of the state or federal constitutions would be precluded.

Amending the U.S. Constitution is very unusual and has been done only to address great public policy need. In

The Federal Marriage Amendment would represent the first time a restriction of the rights of a group of people was written into our Constitution since it was ratified.

214 years, our Constitution has been amended only 17 times since the original Bill of Rights in 1791. Amendments historically have been used to protect or clarify rights and liberties of the American people. The Federal Marriage Amendment would represent the first time a restriction of the rights of a group of people was written into our Constitution since it was ratified in Philadelphia in 1789. (At that time, it contained the notorious "three-fifths" clause, which counted slaves as three-fifths of a person for the purposes of allotting electoral votes. It also excluded women and non–property owners from basic rights.) The FMA would set a significant precedent that would have an enormous impact on the tradition of American justice.

State Marriage Amendments

In 2004, 13 states adopted amendments to their state constitutions to define marriage as exclusively heterosexual. Nine of these 13 amendments also threaten more limited protections. For example, in December 2004, Michigan governor Jean Granholm stripped state employees of domestic partner health coverage, citing the November 2 amendment. Dozens more states will consider such amendments in 2005 and 2006.

HISTORICAL PRECEDENTS TO THE CURRENT DEBATE

A clear parallel to anti-gay marriage activity is the history of bans on interracial marriage. Such marriages evoked social anxieties on the part of some whites that closely parallel those evoked by gay marriage today. In nineteenth-century Tennessee, a black man was charged with criminal fornication with his white wife. The Tennessee Supreme Court rejected the man's defense that the woman was his wife and they had legally married in another state that allowed interracial marriage. Accepting this marriage as valid, the court warned, would lead to condoning pedophilia/incest and polygamy: "the father living with his daughter . . . in lawful wedlock" and "the Turk being allowed to 'establish his harem at the doors of the capitol.'"[36]

In 1912, an amendment was proposed to the U.S. Constitution that would have banned interracial marriage.[37] The next year, Massachusetts passed a law intended to block interracial marriages. The law prevented Massachusetts from marrying couples from out of state whose marriages would not be valid in their home states; this was the case in dozens of states in 1913. In 2004, Massachusetts Attorney General Thomas Reilly said the 1913 law, still on the books, would prevent gay couples from states with anti-gay marriage laws from marrying in Massachusetts.[38]

As recently as 1967, an interracial couple in Virginia were sentenced to one year in jail for violating the state law banning black–white marriages. They could have had their sentence suspended if they agreed to leave the state and not return for 25 years. The trial court appealed to divine guidance: "Almighty God created the races white, black, yellow, Malay and red, and He placed them on separate continents. And but for the interference with His arrangement there would be no cause for such marriages. The fact that He separated the races shows that He did not intend for the races to mix."[39] When the U.S. Supreme Court struck down Virginia's law and those of 15 other states, fewer than 40 years ago, 72% of Americans opposed interracial marriage, and 48% believed it should be a crime.[40]

In 1967, 72% of Americans opposed interracial marrage. 48% of Americans believed interracial marriage should be classified as a crime.

CIVIL MARRIAGE AND RELIGIOUS MARRIAGE

The Massachusetts Court noted that the distinction between civil marriage and religious marriage dates back to the arrival of the first English colonists in Massachusetts: ". . . civil marriage is, and since pre-colonial days has been precisely what its name implies: a wholly secular institution. Civil marriage anchors an ordered society by encouraging stable relationships over transient ones."[41] As Harvard University's Peter Gomes points out, the first Puritans saw civil marriage as "unscriptural," and even after the arrival of the first clergyman, Rev. Ralph Smith, in 1629, marriages were solely civil contracts for more than 50 years of early American history. It was only after the joining of Plymouth Colony with the Massachusetts Bay Colony in 1692 that the clergy were authorized to perform marriages. Gomes notes that "to this day in this Commonwealth the clergy, including those of the [Catholic] archdiocese, solemnize marriage legally as agents of the Commonwealth and by its civil authority. Chapter 207 of the General Laws of Massachusetts tells who may perform such ceremonies."[42]

Legalization of civil marriage for gay couples will not affect whether a religion will or will not perform or recognize certain marriages.

As the Massachusetts example attests, access to civil marriage is completely unrelated to the right of religions to decide whom they will marry. Many legal marriages, such as marriages after divorce or interfaith marriages, are not blessed within particular religious traditions, but the state still recognizes them. Many religions do not recognize same-sex unions. Legalization of civil marriage for gay couples will not affect whether a religion will or will not perform or recognize certain marriages, just as the legalization of civil divorce has not forced the Roman Catholic Church to change its policy in this area. That said, an increasing number of religions, including Reform and Reconstructionist Judaism, Unitarianism, and many United Church of Christ congregations and Quaker groups, conduct same-sex marriages, and some Episcopalian congregations bless same-sex unions, although none of these unions are recognized by U.S. law. In the Catholic Church, there is a strong current of dissent

**Sample Policies That Give
Preferential Treatment to Married Couples**

- Social Security, workers' compensation, and public assistance

- Employment benefits; family and medical leave

- Federal civilian, military service, and veterans' benefits

- Medical, health, and illness benefits (Medicare, Medicaid)

- Estate and taxation benefits

- Immigration and naturalization policy

- Trade, commerce, and intellectual property rights

- Other legal protections (e.g., portability to other jurisdictions)

**Sample Programs and Protections That Give
Preferential Treatment to Married Couples**

- Family benefits for veterans and certain civilian employees, such as Energy Department employees suffering from radiation sickness

- Coverage under the Medicare+ Choice program

- Nutrition services under the Older Americans Act

- Family violence prevention and services; interstate stalking laws

- Eligibility under first-time homebuyer programs

- Supportive housing for the elderly

- Native American and Native Hawaiian housing assistance

- Aid to small businesses

- Immigration and asylum family provisions

- The right to not testify against one's spouse

Why Civil Unions Are Not Enough

The 1,138 federal benefits and protections of marriage are only available to couples that are allowed to legally marry. These include Social Security survivor and spousal benefits, the ability to file a joint tax return, immigration rights, and coverage under the Family and Medical Leave Act. To date, civil unions are not "portable," meaning that when a couple moves to another state, none of the benefits, rights, or responsibilities associated with civil unions move with them. While the federal government is unlikely to recognize same-sex marriages in the short run, a future President and Congress more supportive of equality may move to treat married same-sex couples equally under federal policy. Under the current legal framework—which is based on *marital* status—the only way to extend federal protections associated with marriage to couples who have entered civil unions would be to amend more than 1,000 separate laws and regulations.

Category	Rights & Responsibilities	Marriage	Civil Unions
Social Security & Related Programs	Social Security—survivor benefits; spousal benefits	Yes	No
	Workers' compensation and dependency benefits	Yes	No
	Public assistance benefits—federal housing; food stamp programs	Yes	No
Employment Benefits & Related Laws	Spousal insurance benefits through one's employer	Yes	No
	Unpaid leave in order to care for a sick spouse under federal Family & Medical Leave Act, most state FMLAs	Yes	No
	Wages and retirement benefits for deceased spouse	Yes	No
Federal Civilian, Military Service, & Veteran's Benefits	Veterans' benefits—dependency and indemnity compensation; monthly pension; medical care	Yes	No
	Federal civilian employee and military benefits—health insurance; survivor benefits; pension benefits	Yes	No
Medical, Health & Illness Benefits	Medicare—spousal benefits	Yes	No
	Medicaid—spend-down protection	Yes	No
	Automatic medical decision-making power and hospital visitation rights	Yes	No
	Protections for families of crime victims	Yes	No
Estate & Taxation Benefits	Ability to file joint income tax returns with the IRS	Yes	No
	Unlimited exemptions from federal gift and estate taxes on transfers to spouse	Yes	No
	Inheritance of a share of spouse's estate	Yes	No
	Automatic financial decision-making power on spouse's behalf	Yes	No
Immigration, Naturalization, & Aliens	Petition for spouse to immigrate to the U.S.	Yes	No
	Family reunification for asylees	Yes	No
Trade, Commerce, & Intellectual Property Rights	Ability to file jointly for bankruptcy protection	Yes	No
	Renewal and/or termination rights of copyrighted work of deceased partner	Yes	No
Other Legal Benefits & Protections	Marital communication privilege—right to not testify against one's spouse	Yes	No
	Recognition and guaranteed provision of rights in other jurisdictions	Yes	No
	Coverage under federal law prohibiting discrimination based on legal relationship status	Yes	No

against the hierarchy's active opposition to the legalization of civil marriage for same-sex couples.[43]

Civil marriage provides a comprehensive package of economic and social protections to couples and their children. A 2004 report by the U.S. General Accounting Office lists 1,138 ways in which marital relationships are given special treatment by the federal government.[44] A few of these are listed here.

The federal protections afforded by marriage are important particularly in old age and in times of crisis, such as illness and death. Unequal treatment under Social Security survivor benefits, pensions, and other retirement plans can cost same-sex surviving partners tens and sometimes hundreds of thousands of dollars that could help them in retirement.[45] In addition to these rights, there are hundreds of other rights, benefits, and responsibilities automatically conferred upon married couples that have implications at the local and state level, and in relation to employers and private entities.

"Family Values": A Political Agenda

DEFINING THE ANTI-GAY MOVEMENT

Scholars have described the anti-gay movement in various, overlapping ways. John Green defines the "Christian right" as "a social movement concentrated among Evangelical Protestants and dedicated to restoring 'traditional values' in public policy. . . . Opposition to gay rights was one of the original pillars of the Christian Right."[1] Didi Herman "define[s] the Christian right as a broad coalition of profamily organizations (e.g., Focus on the Family, Concerned Women for America, Traditional Values Coalition) that have come together to struggle for their socio-political vision in the public sphere. These organizations, and their activist leaders, are predominantly committed to a conservative, largely premillenial, Protestant Christianity."[2] In Massachusetts and elsewhere, Roman Catholic church leaders are increasingly joining anti-gay coalitions. For three decades, anti-gay organizing, particularly in the form of local and statewide ballot campaigns, has been a central focus and strategy of these groups.[3]

Abortion remained the central domestic policy issue for the religious right into the 1980s. It was the increased passage of sexual orientation nondiscrimination laws, the promotion of safe-schools initiatives and gay–straight alliances to support gay youth, and public funding of "homoerotic" art that evoked a new surge in anti-gay activism in the late 1980s and early 1990s.[4] Anti-gay organizing and appeals to anti-gay sentiment, which are deeply rooted in American culture,[5] support "the right's movement building," help build "internal movement cohesion," and allow them "to rally the movement, raise money and win recruits," argues Jean Hardisty, a leading scholar of rightwing politics.[6] But it is not solely, cynically instrumental; anti-gay politics reflect a "sincere belief that homosexuality is an abomination because it is a sin against God."[7] The movement's various rallying cries have been successful at, specifically, soliciting considerable financial contributions from supporters. With these resources it is able to wield significant political influence in support of its agenda.

FINANCIAL RESOURCES

Anti-gay groups outspend gay rights organizations by at least a four-to-one ratio.

Anti-gay activists often portray gay people and activists as politically powerful, well-funded elites. For example, Ken Connor of the Family Research Council wrote in a recent fundraising letter: "The Human Rights Campaign and the other groups in the homosexual lobby have very deep pockets. Big corporations, elite foundations, and Hollywood celebrities underwrite the homosexual lobby with tens of millions of dollars every year."[8] Traditional Values Coalition Executive Director Andrea Sheldon slammed President Clinton for speaking at a Human Rights Campaign dinner in 1997, denouncing "an American President kissing up to the wealthiest extremists of the left."[9] However, anti-gay groups actually outspend gay rights organizations by at least a four-to-one ratio.

Twenty-nine groups cosponsored the anti-gay "Marriage Protection Week" held in October 2003, which promoted the Federal Marriage Amendment and opposition to any benefits or protections for same-sex couples, even domestic partner health insurance. Of these 29 groups, recent income data was available for 13 of them; these 13 groups shared a combined annual income of $217 million. This compared to just $54 million for the 13 *largest* national gay political organizations.[10]

In Massachusetts, four national anti-gay groups are heavily involved in the fight against same-sex marriage,

Annual Income of 13 "Marriage Protection Week" Sponsors vs. 13 Largest National Gay Rights Advocacy Organizations

13 Sponsors of Marriage Protection Week for Which Income Data Is Publicly Available

Focus on the Family	www.family.org	$126,251,827
Prison Fellowship	www.pfm.org	46,310,285
American Family Association	www.afa.net	14,072,427
Concerned Women for America (CWA)	www.cwfa.org	11,999,881
Family Research Council	www.frc.org	9,730,169
Free Congress Foundation	www.freecongress.org	*2,680,004
Nat'l Coalition for the Protection of Children & Families	www.nationalcoalition.org	1,577,827
Eagle Forum	www.eagleforum.org	**1,569,697
Americans United for Life	www.unitedforlife.org	**1,118,102
American Values	www.ouramericanvalues.org	870,141
Traditional Values Coalition	www.traditionalvalues.org	**581,783
American Cause	www.theamericancause.org	**415,003
Citizens for Community Values	www.ccv.org	**89,388
Total		**$217,266,534**

13 Largest National Gay, Lesbian, Bisexual and Transgender Advocacy Organizations

Human Rights Campaign/HRC Foundation	www.hrc.org	**$17,334,997
Lambda Legal Defense and Education Fund, Inc.	www.lambdalegal.org	9,509,686
Gay and Lesbian Alliance Against Defamation, Inc.	www.glaad.org	5,300,000
National Gay & Lesbian Task Force/NGLTF Foundation	www.ngltf.org	***5,121,163
Gay, Lesbian, & Straight Education Network	www.glsen.org	3,325,203
LLEGO (National Latino/a Lesbian & Gay Organization)	www.llego.org	2,500,000
Parents & Friends of Lesbians and Gay Men	www.pflag.org	**2,363,005
Victory Fund/Foundation	www.victoryfund.org	2,000,000
Servicemember's Legal Defense Network	www.sldn.org	1,800,000
National Center for Lesbian Rights	www.nclrights.org	**1,414,120
International Gay & Lesbian Human Rights Commission	www.iglhrc.org	1,357,355
Freedom to Marry Collaborative	www.freedomtomarry.org	****1,100,000
National Youth Advocacy Coalition	www.nyacyouth.org	1,021,907
Total		**$54,147,436**

Information retrieved from Guidestar.org (IRS 990 forms), unless otherwise noted.
*2000 Revenues
**2001 Revenues
***FY2002–2003 Audited Financial Statement
****2003 Approved Budget

Source: Cahill, S., Cianciotto, J., Colvin, R., Johnson-Lashley, N., & Roberts F. (2003). *"Marriage Protection Week" sponsors: Are they really interested in "building strong and healthy marriages?"* New York: Policy Institute of the National Gay and Lesbian Task Force.

ANNUAL INCOME ANALYSIS

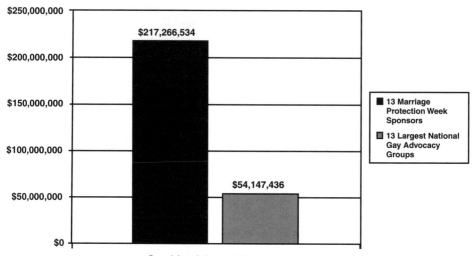

In Massachusetts anti-gay forces out-resource pro-gay forces by a ratio of more than five to one.

joining 11 local groups such as the Black Ministerial Alliance of Greater Boston and the Massachusetts Catholic Conference under the rubric of the Coalition for Marriage. Annual budget data was available for nine of the 15 members of the anti-gay Coalition for Marriage. The combined annual income for these nine groups is $168 million a year. By contrast, income data was available for 16 out of 18 member organizations of MassEquality, a pro-gay marriage coalition. The combined annual income for these 16 groups is $27 million a year. Thus, in Massachusetts anti-gay forces out-resource pro-gay forces by a ratio of more than five to one.[11] In both the anti-gay and pro-gay coalitions a few large national groups' budgets make up the lion's share of resources.

LOCAL CAMPAIGNS

Many of the groups promoting the Federal Marriage Amendment and the many state constitutional amendments banning marriage and other forms of partner recognition around the country have been deeply involved in local and statewide ballot campaigns since at least 1992. While they often work with a local group that promotes itself as grassroots, in fact much of the campaign's resources come from the national anti-gay groups. Concerned Women for America, Eagle Forum, Focus on the Family, and the Traditional Values Coalition all served on the executive and advisory boards of Colorado for Family Values in 1992. Today, all are backing the Federal Marriage Amendment, and all but Eagle Forum are heavily involved in the fight against gay marriage in Massachusetts.

The Christian Coalition had a strong presence in Colorado's successful anti-gay ballot campaign in 1992 and in other anti-gay ballot campaigns.[12] The Oregon Citizens' Alliance, promoter of dozens of successful anti-gay ballot questions in the late 1980s and early 1990s, is a local affiliate of the Christian Coalition. The Massachusetts Family Institute, which is leading the fight against gay marriage there, is a state affiliate of Focus on the Family.[13] And the Christian Coalition has been active in many other locales: defeating the multicultural "Children of the Rainbow" curriculum in New York City in 1991, which it conflated with another proposed sex education curriculum aimed at older students to accuse the school chancellor of "teaching sodomy to kindergarten students"; defeating a gay member of the Des Moines, Iowa, school board in 1995; and repealing through a 1998 referendum a statewide sexual orientation law passed by the Maine legislature in 1997.[14]

Today in Massachusetts, a number of national anti-gay groups are centrally involved in the struggle to outlaw marriage for same-sex couples. Concerned Women for America, Focus on the Family, the Traditional Values Coalition, and the Family Research Council are members of the Coalition for Marriage, along with the Massachusetts Family Institute and several local groups.[15] The Coalition for Marriage, an umbrella group comprised of these organizations and others, is primarily focused on preventing the legalization of same-sex marriage in Massachusetts. It also opposes more limited forms of partner recognition, such as domestic partnership, arguing, inaccurately, that this is just marriage by another name. The Massachusetts Family Institute's website has links to most of the national anti-gay organizations.

A LARGER AGENDA

Many of the groups leading the fight against gay marriage oppose any form of legal equality for gay people, including nondiscrimination laws, domestic partner benefits and civil unions, safe-schools initiatives aimed at stopping anti-gay harassment, and hate crime laws. They use language that explicitly promotes intolerance and discrimination against gay people, including gay youth in the schools. For example, the Traditional Values Coalition affirms that "we believe in intolerance to those things that are evil; and we believe that we should discriminate against those behaviors which are dangerous to individuals and to society."[16] The American Family Association, a cosponsor of Marriage Protection Week and the Federal Marriage Amendment, opposes efforts to end widespread anti-gay harassment and violence in schools.[17]

Many groups opposing same-sex marriage promote an even broader agenda. Several of the groups cosponsoring Marriage Protection Week have led the fight against affirmative action, reproductive choice, immigration, benefits for legal Mexican workers, and the Equal Rights Amendment. For example, American Cause, led by Pat Buchanan, opposes affirmative action and abortion rights. Buchanan calls "mass immigration" a "suicide pill of the GOP."[18] The Traditional Values Coalition, Focus on the Family, Concerned Women for America, and Eagle Forum oppose reproductive choice, the teaching of evolution in public schools, and comprehensive sex education. They also promote prayer in public schools.[19] The Family Research Council supports a school prayer amendment to the U.S. Constitution and would like to abolish the U.S. Department of Education (DOE).[20] Concerned Women for America also seeks the abolition of the DOE.[21] Before Ron Crews took the helm of the Massachusetts Family Institute, he served as a Georgia state legislator and then as the Georgia Christian Coalition's legislative director. He lobbied the Georgia Department of Education to teach creationism in the classroom, without success.[22]

The Family Research Council promotes an end to no-fault divorce and the requirement of mutual consent for divorce, as well as "covenant marriage" laws now in effect in Louisiana, Arizona, and Arkansas.[23] Covenant marriages are much harder to enter into and harder to dissolve.[24] When Tony Perkins, now head of the Family Research Council, was a Republican State Representative in Louisiana, he drafted the first covenant marriage law, passed in 1997. A Family Research Council document states:

> . . . after consulting with . . . a group of pastors in his district . . . [Perkins] drafted a bill that only allowed for divorce in what they saw as the biblically licit cases of adultery and abandonment. Perkins said he wanted to start with a high standard, the biblical ideal for marriage, because he knew that he would have to compromise in the legislative process.[25]

It is important to note that spousal abuse is not listed as a "biblically licit" reason for divorce.

Many groups opposing same-sex marriage have led the fight against affirmative action, reproductive choice, immigration benefits for legal Mexican workers, and the Equal Rights Amendment.

FOCUS ON HOMOSEXUALITY

According to the National Center for Health at the U.S. Department of Health and Human Services, many factors correlate with marital breakdown (divorce) or failure to marry, including lack of access to quality education, low family income, and unemployment: "First marriages are more likely to disrupt in communities with higher unemployment, lower median family income, and a higher percentage of families below poverty level or receiving public assistance."[26]

Anti-gay marriage groups pay much less attention to poverty (affecting nearly one in five U.S. children), the increasing rate of families without health insurance,[27] domestic violence,[28] failure to pay child support, or other issues. The disproportionate focus on homosexuality is reflected in a content analysis of the websites of key Marriage Protection Week sponsors. Of the 29 organizations cosponsoring Marriage Protection Week, nine had websites that allow users to search all of the documents available on the site. Searches using a few keywords found that these nine groups mentioned *homosexual* in a total of 2,369 documents, but *divorce* was mentioned in only 1,432 documents. *Poverty* was mentioned in 832 documents, *health insurance* in 207 documents, *domestic violence* in 190 documents, and *child support* in only 85 documents.[29]

In a search of nine "pro-family" organization websites, *homosexual* appears nearly twice as often as *divorce*, nearly four times as often as *poverty*, and more than ten times as often as the terms *health insurance* and *domestic violence*.

WHAT DO ANTI-GAY GROUPS SAY ABOUT SAME-SEX MARRIAGE AND GAY FAMILIES?

Anti-gay family activists are widely quoted in the media, and their claims are taken up by media commentators and anti-gay politicians. Some of their arguments have been particularly effective in blocking proposed policy changes that would provide protections or legal equality for gay people. Given the success the anti-gay movement has had in promoting anti-gay marriage laws and amendments in 40 states, and given that dozens of states have recently passed or currently are considering anti-gay family constitutional amendments, it is extremely important for the public to be aware of the claims made and of the facts behind them. Here are some of the most frequently made (and most frequently damaging) claims, and the truth behind the myths.

1. ALLOWING GAY COUPLES TO MARRY WILL DAMAGE OR DESTROY THE INSTITUTION OF MARRIAGE.

Anti-gay family groups warn that allowing same-sex couples to marry will hurt or even destroy marriage for heterosexual couples. They argue that the high divorce rate (about half of U.S. marriages end in divorce), marital infidelity, the increased prevalence of nonmarital births, widespread cohabitation by unmarried straight couples, and pornography have already weakened marriage, and that allowing gay couples to marry will be the straw that breaks the camel's back. The Coalition for Marriage warns that "legalizing same-sex marriage means both the definition of marriage and the institution of marriage will be destructively eroded, with enormous negative implications for society and the common good."[30] The Traditional Values Coalition's director Rev. Lou Sheldon warned in a September 2003 fundraising letter that "this flood tide of perversion" of "homosexual activists" seeks to "abolish the idea of marriage altogether."[31] Maggie Gallagher of the Institute for American Values warned that "the great threat unisex marriage poses to marriage as a social institution . . . is an abyss at our feet . . . a disaster."[32] Conservative politicians repeatedly echo these claims.[33]

Such claims are simply not warranted. Other than repeatedly asserting that allowing gay couples to marry would undermine or hurt marriage, anti-gay activists, politicians, and opinion leaders have not presented any

Anti-gay activists, politicians, and opinion leaders have not presented any evidence that damage would be done to the institution of marriage if gay couples are allowed to marry.

evidence, nor have they constructed a compelling argument, that damage would be done to the institution of marriage if gay couples are allowed to marry. In fact, U.S. Census data indicate divorce rates are lowest in Massachusetts—home of the only legal same-sex marriage in the United States in 2004—and highest in the Bible Belt states of the deep South.[34] Allowing committed same-sex partners to marry will help them protect their families and will hurt no more than allowing people of different races or religions to marry, or allowing divorced people to marry again, has injured civil society.

2. GAY RELATIONSHIPS ARE UNHEALTHY.

The Family Research Council claims that "homosexual relationships are harmful . . . their consequences are far more negative than positive."[35] Therefore, the state should not encourage same-sex relationships, which legalizing marriage would allegedly do: "Society grants benefits to marriage because marriage has benefits for society—including, but not limited to, the reproduction of the species. . . . Homosexual relationships, on the other hand, have no comparable benefit for society, and in fact impose substantial costs on society. The fact that AIDS is at least ten times more common among men who have sex with men than among the general population is but one example."[36]

Studies show that gay and lesbian couples are comparable to opposite-sex couples in many ways, and that relationship quality and satisfaction are about the same across all couple types (straight, gay, lesbian).[37] Although some gay relationships do not work out, this is also true of many heterosexual relationships. Many same-sex couples share their lives together and care for one another, and an increasing number raise children together. They struggle to

In the U.K. and several European countries, 59% of new HIV cases diagnosed between 1997 and 2001 occurred through heterosexual sex. In the U.S., most reported HIV infections among 13- to 19-year-olds were among women and girls, most of whom were infected heterosexually.

make ends meet, to remain faithful to each other, to create a loving home, and to participate as members of society. It is true that gay and bisexual men are at higher risk of HIV in the United States. In Africa and much of the rest of the world, however, HIV is more likely to be transmitted through heterosexual sex than through homosexual sex. This is also true of most new HIV transmissions among U.S. teens. Intravenous drug use and poor health care are also key correlates of HIV risk.[38] In the U.S., lesbians are at lower risk for HIV than heterosexual men and women.[39] Again, no one argues that straight men and women should be denied rights because they are at higher risk for AIDS than lesbians. Because lesbians are half of the homosexual population, the claim that gay and lesbian families are socially undesirable because of the higher prevalence of AIDS among gay men is not tenable.

3. GAY RELATIONSHIPS ARE UNSAFE.

The Family Research Council (FRC) and the Massachusetts Family Institute (MFI) claim that gay and lesbian couples experience twice as much domestic violence as heterosexual couples. FRC does not provide a citation for this claim beyond a vague reference to "government statistics."[40] MFI also warns that "homosexual marriage would affirm violent behavior: the incidence of domestic violence among gay men is nearly double that in the heterosexual population."[41] MFI does not cite original research from a peer-reviewed academic journal, nor does it cite government data. Instead, it cites a 2001 Family Research Council report titled *Preserving Marriage in an Age of Counterfeits: How "Civil Unions" Devalue the Real Thing.*[42]

While many gay men and lesbians have experienced domestic violence, so too have many heterosexuals, particularly women. (Of course, bisexuals are found in both same-sex and opposite-sex relationships.) A 1998

"Same-sex battering mirrors heterosexual battering both in type and prevalence."

Commonwealth Fund survey found that one in three American women report being raped and/or physically assaulted by a current or former boyfriend at some point in their lives.[43] According to this study, one in three U.S. women experiences domestic abuse or sexual assault at the hands of her male partner during her lifetime. This is a higher rate of domestic violence than that reported by gay men in a Boston study (which reported one in four gay men had experienced domestic violence at some point in their lives),[44] and in the middle of the range reported for lesbians in a number of studies.[45] According to the American Bar Association, based on cases that have been prosecuted, "same-sex battering mirrors heterosexual battering both in type and prevalence."[46] The U.S. Department of Justice does not separate out same-sex domestic violence from opposite-sex domestic violence in its statistics.[47]

The claim that gay relationships are more likely to experience domestic violence than heterosexual relationships is false. Relationship violence is a social problem that should be prevented through education and punished through fair and vigorous enforcement of the law. It is not a justification for denying a class of people basic rights.

4. BECAUSE GAY PEOPLE AND THEIR RELATIONSHIPS ARE UNHEALTHY AND DESTRUCTIVE, THEY ARE A DRAIN ON THE ECONOMY.

To the contrary, gay couple families have been proven to contribute a great deal to society and to the economy. A comparison of the same-sex households who self-identified on the 2000 Census with married opposite-sex couple households in Massachusetts found that gay couples in Massachusetts were more likely to hold a bachelor's or graduate degree than married straight couples, more likely to work in the private sector, and "clearly contribute valuable skills to the economic vitality of the state." Nearly three quarters (73.3%) were property owners, compared with 80% of married opposite-sex couples. The value of their homes and median and mean income were slightly below those of married straight couples, but this could be a function of age, as the average age of gay partners was 43 years, while the average age of married opposite-sex partners was 49.[48] A 2001 Brookings Institution study found a correlation between large and fast-growing high technology sectors and the presence of concentrations of gay and lesbian people in metropolitan areas. According to economist Richard Florida, "high levels of tolerance that attract gay people also appear to attract talented and well-educated workers, the group that is required for economic growth."[49] Around the country, municipalities both large and small are looking to Florida's research as a valuable new key to encouraging and sustaining economic and cultural vitality.

"High levels of tolerance that attract gay people also appear to attract talented and well-educated workers, the group that is required for economic growth."

5. GAY PARENTING IS A LOOMING THREAT THAT ENDANGERS CHILDREN AND SOCIETY.

Many anti-gay groups, such as the Coalition for Marriage, discuss gay parenting in the abstract, as if it is a possible future phenomenon and not a current reality for thousands of gay and lesbian families. In a full-page ad that appeared in the *Boston Globe* on January 23, 2004, Focus on the Family implied that gay marriage would lead to gay parenting in the future, not that it would protect existing lesbian and gay families raising children: "Same-sex marriage advocates and the Massachusetts Supreme Judicial Court are asking our state and nation to enter a massive, untested social experiment with coming generations of children. We must ask one simple question: Is the same-sex 'family' good for children?" The ad conflates gay and lesbian parenting with

Research overwhelmingly indicates that children raised by two gay and lesbian parents are not disadvantaged vis-à-vis their peers raised by heterosexual parents.

fatherlessness, since "most children growing up in same-sex homes are living with two women." It then claims that "children in mother-only homes suffer harmful consequences" from father absence, including "lower physical health" and emotional health; higher risk of abuse; lower school performance; lower self-confidence, compassion, and respect for women; and "higher criminal behavior" and "higher sexual experimentation."

Single-parent families are most at risk for poverty and related problems, due to poor public policy decisions.

Concerned Women for America's Robert Knight said that Ontario's June 2003 landmark high court ruling in favor of same-sex marriage did a "great disservice to children."[50] The Massachusetts-focused Coalition for Marriage claims, without citing research, that "the children who will be raised by same-sex parents will more closely resemble the children raised by a single parent than they will the children raised by their two biological parents."[51] The Coalition notes that children raised in single-parent homes are more likely to experience behavioral problems and problems in school, and are more likely to be abused. However, poverty and other factors are significant correlates to these problems; and the high extra-marital birthrate in Europe shows that nonmarital births do not necessarily cause problems in a child's development. Such simplistic and inaccurate causal claims stigmatize not only gay parents, but millions of single and unmarried parents.[52]

6. GAY PARENTS ARE MORE LIKELY TO ABUSE THEIR CHILDREN.

Focus on the Family, the largest cosponsor of Marriage Protection Week, and the Coalition for Marriage imply that having two gay fathers or two lesbian mothers makes children more susceptible to child abuse, a claim that is not supported by credible social science research. An August 2003 briefing paper on same-sex marriage distributed by Focus on the Family states, "Same-sex parenting situations make it impossible for a child to live with both biological parents, thus increasing their risk of abuse."[53]

Boston's Catholic Archbishop Sean O'Malley warns that legalizing gay marriage "would worsen the breakdown of the American family and exacerbate the problems of poverty, child abuse, and human suffering already wrought by 'widespread cohabitation and galloping divorce rates.'"[54] Earlier in 2003, the Vatican issued a statement accusing gay and lesbian parents of "doing violence" to their children by virtue of being gay.[55]

In fact, as the research cited in chapter 3 shows, children raised by gay and lesbian parents are not disadvantaged vis-à-vis their peers raised by heterosexual parents.[56] Instead, a wide body of research shows that children of lesbian and gay parents thrive in loving homes. The policy response to claims that gay parents "do violence" to their children by virtue of being gay would require the state to take children away from their gay and lesbian parents. This would not only hurt children in caring families and current and prospective gay parents, but also children in need of loving homes. At least 110,000 children are waiting to be adopted in the U.S.[57] But in 1997, there were qualified adoptive parents available for only 20,000 of them.[58] Approximately 588,000 children are currently in foster care.[59] Children who remain in foster care for much of their childhood, as do tens of thousands of American children, are more likely to have emotional problems, delinquency, substance abuse, and academic problems. Some children in foster care live in 20 or more homes by the time they reach the age of 18.[60] Barring gay men and lesbians from adopting or foster parenting is not simply unjust and unethical; it also decreases the number of potential suitable homes for children in need.

At least 110,000 children are waiting to be adopted in the U.S. Approximately 588,000 children are currently in foster care. Barring gay men and lesbians from adopting or foster parenting decreases the number of potential suitable homes for children in need.

7. GAY MEN ARE MORE LIKELY
TO BE PEDOPHILES.

Perhaps the most egregious and damaging claim promulgated by anti-gay groups is the claim that homosexuality is intrinsically linked to pedophilia and child sexual abuse. The Family Research Council (FRC) notes that "almost all child sexual abuse is committed by men" and claims that "less than 3 percent of American men identity themselves as homosexual; yet nearly a third of all cases of child sexual abuse are homosexual in nature [that is, they involve men molesting boys]. This is a rate of homosexual child abuse about ten times higher than one would expect based on the first two facts." This is evidence, FRC claims, that "homosexuality is a significant risk factor for this horrible crime."[61] FRC's website promotes a number of reports portraying homosexuality as intrinsically connected to child sexual abuse and as a threat to children: these include "Homosexuality and Child Sexual Abuse" and "Homosexual Parenting: Placing Children at Risk."[62] The Traditional Values Coalition (TVC) claims that "since homosexual couples can't reproduce, they will simply go after *your* children for seduction and conversion to homosexuality. . . . As homosexuals continue to make inroads into public schools, more children will be molested and indoctrinated into the world of homosexuality. Many of them will die in that world."[63]

A 1998 study in the *Journal of the American Medical Association* found that 90% of pedophiles are men, and 95% of these individuals are heterosexual.

The view that gay people are an intrinsic or disproportionate threat to children persists in the highest decision-making circles of the government. During the March 2003 Supreme Court hearing on a challenge to the Texas sodomy law, Chief Justice Rehnquist asked whether an equal protection finding would require municipalities to hire gay people as kindergarten teachers, as if gays are an intrinsic threat to five-year-olds. Scalia mentioned this in his dissent in *Lawrence*, joined by Rehnquist: "Many Americans do not want persons who openly engage in homosexual conduct as partners in their business, as scoutmasters for their children, as teachers in their children's schools or as boarders in their home," Scalia wrote. "They view this as protecting themselves and their families from a lifestyle that they believe to be immoral and destructive."

The social science research on sexual orientation and child sexual abuse clearly disproves the claim that homosexuals are more likely to molest children. A 1998 study in the *Journal of the American Medical Association* found that 90% of pedophiles are men, and 95% of these individuals are heterosexual.[64] One researcher explained this statistic by noting, "Gay men desire consensual sexual relations with other adult men. Pedophiles are usually adult men who are sexually attracted to pre-pubescent children. They are rarely sexually attracted to other adults."[65] In fact, research has indicated that gay men and lesbians are *less* likely than heterosexuals to sexually abuse children. Two studies that examined the sexual orientation of convicted child molesters found that less than 1% in one study and 0% in the other were lesbian or gay.[66] One psychologist reviewed the existing social science literature on the relationship between sexuality and child sexual abuse and found that "a gay man is no more likely than a straight man to perpetrate sexual activity with children."[67] Further, "cases of perpetration of sexual behavior with a pre-pubescent child by an adult lesbian are virtually nonexistent."[68]

Gay rights activists, like all advocates for children's welfare, oppose child sexual abuse and support equitable age of consent laws that help prevent and punish such abuse.[69]

Research has indicated that gay men and lesbians are less likely than heterosexuals to sexually abuse children.

8. GAY MARRIAGE IS A THREAT TO RELIGIOUS FREEDOM; RELIGIONS WILL BE FORCED TO RECOGNIZE AND SANCTION GAY UNIONS.

During the 1996 Defense of Marriage Act debate, Concerned Women for America falsely claimed that conservative religious congregations would be forced to marry same-sex couples if same-sex marriage was legalized.[70] Similar claims were made by Massachusetts legislators opposed to same-sex marriage during a March 29, 2004, debate. In fact, the legalization of gay marriage under civil marriage laws in the U.S. would not change the religious freedom of conservative congregations to refuse to marry gay couples, just as the legalization of divorce does not prevent the Catholic Church from maintaining its policy of not recognizing divorces or second marriages of divorced Catholics who do not obtain an annulment.

9. GAY RIGHTS ADVANCES ARE AKIN TO TERRORISM.

Several of the groups opposing marriage equality have used the vocabulary of terrorism to talk about gay rights advances, invoking comparisons with 9/11 and al-Qaeda.

Several of the groups opposing marriage equality have compared gay rights advances to terrorism. The Traditional Values Coalition's Lou Sheldon compared the June 2003 U.S. Supreme Court ruling striking down sodomy laws to the 9/11 terrorist attacks, and either gays or the Supreme Court to the terrorists who struck that day:

> This is a major wake-up call. This is a 9/11, major wake-up call that the enemy is at our doorsteps. This decision will open a floodgate. This will redirect the stream of what is morally right and what is morally wrong into a deviant kind of behavior. There is no way that homosexuality can be seen other than [as] a social disorder.[71]

Concerned Women for America warned in a September 2003 press release that same-sex marriage "pose[s] a new threat to U.S. border security" and referred to a legally married Canadian same-sex couple trying to enter the U.S. as a married couple as "the latest pair of 'domestic terrorists.'"[72] Raymond Flynn of Your Catholic Voice and Tony Perkins of the Family Research Council compared the Massachusetts high court ruling to terrorism.

An essay posted on the Massachusetts Family Institute website compares gay couples seeking to marry and Democrats who support them to a domestic al-Qaeda. Dennis Prager argues that "The war over same-sex marriage and the war against Islamic totalitarianism are actually two fronts in the same war—a war for the preservation of the unique creation known as Judeo-Christian civilization."[73]

10. SAME-SEX MARRIAGE SIGNALS THE BREAKDOWN OF SOCIETY AND IS PART OF A SATANIC PLOT TO DESTROY CIVILIZATION.

Sandy Rios, spokeswoman for Concerned Women for America, has said, "Gay marriage is not the wave of the future . . . it is the precursor of the end of society as we know it, filled not with order and prosperity but with moral chaos and decline."[74] In this 2003 statement, Rios references earlier, more explicit claims that homosexuals represent the forces of darkness.[75] In the anti-gay literature of the 1980s and 1990s, the gay agenda was said to be "symbolic of the all-encompassing plan of the kingdom of darkness as a whole."[76] Pat Robertson has explicitly linked homosexuality to the "antichrist."[77]

As John Green notes, the anti-gay, religious right movement "arose in the late 1970s in response to perceptions of 'moral decay' in American society. Chief among the 'decaying traditions' was the patriarchal family. . . .

Many gay people are deeply religious or spiritual. In one study, 85% of 2,645 African American gay people reported a religious affiliation.

Changes in women's roles, the legalization of abortion, and the spread of sexual permissiveness were central to this perception of moral decay."[78]

Gays are not in league with Satan. Like straight people, they have varying beliefs; many are atheists or agnostics, while many others are deeply religious or spiritual. For example, 85% of 2,645 African American gay people surveyed in summer 2000 reported a religious affiliation. Only 15% indicated they were atheist/agnostic or skipped the question.[79] Many who are religious also believe strongly in secularism and church–state separation.

11. GAY COUPLES DO NOT NEED THE LEGAL PROTECTIONS OF MARRIAGE.

Opponents of marriage equality claim that gay couples do not really need the protections marriage could afford them. The Family Research Council (FRC) says, "the idea that homosexuals are routinely denied the right to visit their partners in the hospital is nonsense." It surveyed hospital administrators who "could not recall a single case" and "were incredulous that this would even be considered an issue."[80]

In fact, partners without legal familial ties are routinely prevented from visiting their partners in hospitals. Here are two recent examples:

- Bill Flanigan was prevented from visiting his life partner, Robert Daniel, when Daniel was dying in a Baltimore hospital in October 2000. Hospital personnel refused to acknowledge that Flanigan and Daniel were family. "Bill and Bobby were soulmates and one of the best couples I've known," said Grace Daniel, Robert's mother. "They loved each other, took care of each other, came to family holidays as a couple, and Bill still babysits for my grandson. If that isn't family, then something is very wrong. When someone is dying, hospitals should be bringing families together rather than keeping them apart."[81]

- Hillary Goodridge, who along with her partner, Julie Goodridge, was the lead plaintiff in the landmark *Goodridge v. Department of Public Health* ruling, experienced a "nightmare" after Julie gave birth to their daughter Annie eight years ago. According to the Associated Press: "After Annie emerged from Julie Goodridge's womb by cesarean section with lungs full of liquid, the infant was rushed from the operating room into intensive care, put on a ventilator and strapped to splints with intravenous tubes inserted in her tiny arms. As Julie's lesbian partner, Hillary, ran frantically from floor to floor between the neonatal unit and post-op, where doctors were sewing up Julie, she was barred at different times from both Julie's and Annie's bedsides by hospital staff because she wasn't legally connected to either. She eventually saw both—by tearfully pleading with a nurse in one instance and telling staff she was Julie's sister in another—but the experience later fueled the couple's determination to make marriage an option for gays and lesbians like themselves."[82]

Partners without legal familial ties are routinely prevented from visiting their loved ones in hospitals.

The FRC also claims that few children would benefit from their gay or lesbian parents' ability to marry: "far fewer homosexual couples than heterosexual ones are raising children at all, for the obvious reason that they are incapable of natural reproduction."[83] In fact, the 2000 Census indicates that lesbian couples parent at about three-quarters the rate of married straight couples, and gay male couples parent at about half the rate. Fewer homosexual couples are raising kids, but not "far fewer."

12. GAY PEOPLE CAN
ALREADY GET MARRIED.

Anti-gay groups insist that allowing gay couples to marry represents granting gay people a special right on top of the right they already have. "Homosexuals in Massachusetts have had the same right to marry as heterosexuals—the right to marry a person of the opposite sex," writes Concerned Women for America's Jan LaRue.[84] The Family Research Council compares laws restricting marriage to opposite-sex couples to laws preventing cousins from marrying and laws preventing adults from marrying children: "Every person, regardless of sexual preference, is legally barred from marrying a child, a close blood relative, a person who is already married, or a person of the same sex. There is no discrimination here, nor does such a policy deny anyone the 'equal protection of the laws' [as guaranteed by the Constitution], since these restrictions apply equally to every individual."[85] In other words, since a gay man could marry a woman, and a lesbian could marry a man (as many gay people have done—often resulting in unhappy and dysfunctional marriages), they have the right to marry. But for a person who is only attracted to and capable of falling in love with someone of the same sex, such freedom is meaningless. For gay people, this right is restrictive rather than liberating, as it limits their ability to protect their life-partner relationships.

Claims that gay people have the same right to marry as straight people rely heavily upon the correlated claim that gay people can change if they really want to, if they try hard enough, and, usually, if they accept Jesus Christ as their savior. This is the rationale behind the "ex-gay" movement.[86] While this may work for a small percentage of individuals, many of whom are likely bisexual and not exclusively homosexual in orientation, it is not something most gay people are capable of or even want to do.

13. GAYS SEEK TO LEGALIZE POLYGAMY OR GROUP MARRIAGE.

Anti-gay groups warn that those seeking to legalize marriage for same-sex couples are also seeking the legalization of marriages between three or more people. Lou Sheldon predicted that the legalization of same-sex marriage would lead to marriages between "three women and two men, or two women and three men."[87] The Traditional Values Coalition's website claims, "Homosexual activists . . . don't want to marry just to have a normal home life. They want same-sex marriage as a way of destroying the concept of marriage altogether—and of introducing polygamy and polyamory [group sex] as 'families.' . . . Their ultimate goal is to abolish all prohibitions against sex with multiple partners."[88] A flyer for Marriage Protection Week in October 2003 claimed that those seeking government recognition of same-sex marriages also want the government to recognize polygamous marriages: "Homosexual activists have made great progress toward redefining marriage to include two men, two women or a group of any size or mix of sexes."[89] The Family Research Council and Concerned Women for America have made similar claims. The Family Research Council's Robert Knight recently warned that if same-sex marriage is allowed, "other groups, such as bisexuals and polygamists, will demand the right to redefine marriage to suit their own proclivities. Once the standard of one-man, one-woman marriage is broken, there is no logical stopping point."[90]

There are many falsehoods in these statements. Marriage equality advocates are not seeking recognition of marriages between more than two individuals. The conflation of bisexuality with promiscuity is a common misperception. Bisexuals are found both in heterosexual relationships and in homosexual relationships. Many

There is no evidence that bisexuals are any more or less promiscuous than other people.

people perceived to be straight or gay are in fact able to be attracted to both men and women. There is no evidence that bisexuals are any more or less promiscuous than other people.[91] Polygamy was banned by the federal government more than a century ago, and the ban has never been challenged by gay activist groups.

14. GAY MARRIAGE THREATENS ACCEPTED GENDER ROLES AND WILL LEAD TO A DECLINE IN THE POPULATION.

Focus on the Family (FOF) warned that the *Goodridge* ruling would encourage "too much same-sex coupling," which "will threaten the creation and development of the next generation." FOF claimed that, while there can never be "too much" heterosexual marriage, "society can suffer from too much homosexual marriage," which "will also threaten the necessary values of monogamy, the social necessity of men caring for and protecting women and women domesticating men. These important tasks will become optional."[92] Such stereotypical understandings of gender roles and the roles of husbands and wives are typical of the anti-gay groups' worldview. These claims illustrate Suzanne Pharr's claim that anti-gay bias is closely connected to sexism.

The Benefits of Being Family

DEFINING THE FAMILY

The vast majority of policies that govern family life in this country begin with the idea that a family is a unit comprised of a married man and woman and their biological children. But such a limited definition is out of touch with the contemporary demographic reality of American families. Almost one-third of families with children in the United States are headed by either single parents or two unmarried, cohabiting parents.[1] Approximately 44% of adults in the United States are unmarried. Married heterosexual couples with children comprise less than one-quarter of American households, according to the 2000 U.S. Census.[2]

Most lesbians and gay men aspire to have committed, loving relationships and want a stronger sense of family in their lives.[3] Although demographic research on gay, lesbian, and bisexual people is limited, and most national surveys do not ask about sexual orientation, there is a significant body of research from which we can discern some trends. A series of studies from the 1970s to the 1990s found that between 64% and 80% of lesbians and 46% to 60% of gay men report that they are in committed partner relationships.[4] Studies show that gay and lesbian relationships are comparable to opposite-sex relationships in terms of quality of the relationship and satisfaction in the relationship.[5] Contrary to common misconceptions, many lesbian and gay couples are raising children, as are thousands of single gay parents.

Concentration of Same-Sex Couples: Florida

Source: Bradford, J., Barrett, K., and Honnold, J. A. (2002). *The 2000 Census and Same-Sex Households: A User's Guide.* New York: The National Gay and Lesbian Task Force Policy Institute, the Survey and Evaluation Research Laboratory, and The Fenway Institute.

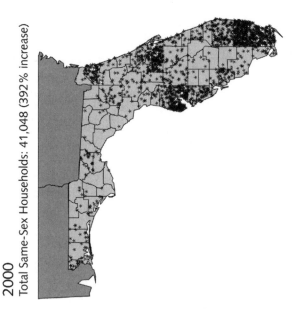

2000
Total Same-Sex Households: 41,048 (392% increase)

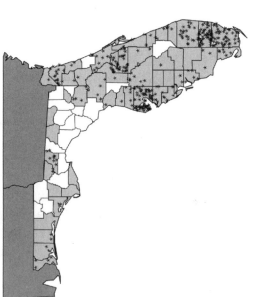

1990
Total Same-Sex Households: 8,492

* = 25 same-sex households

counties reporting one or more same-sex households

counties reporting zero same-sex households

THE 2000 CENSUS'S SAME-SEX COUPLE SAMPLE

The existence and widespread distribution of same-sex couples is reflected in the 2000 Census data, in which nearly 600,000 same-sex cohabiting couples self-reported as "unmarried partners." Although this number likely represents a significant undercount, it constitutes a 310% increase over the 145,130 same-sex households tallied in the 1990 Census.[6] If gay and lesbian people represent about 5% of the U.S. population,[7] as a broad range of surveys indicate, and roughly three-fifths to two-thirds are in partnered relationships, as studies indicate, it is likely that approximately three million same-sex couples exist in the U.S. However, this is a very rough estimate, and the actual number could be significantly different.

Unfortunately, the Census does not allow us to identify many gay people, including those who are single, those whose partners have died, and people who are in a long-term same-sex relationship but who are not cohabiting with their partner. Many gay couples may have chosen not to indicate that they were "unmarried partners" because they didn't want the government to have this information. In a country where gay people were defined as criminals under the sodomy laws on the books in 13 states until June 2003, and in which the government continues to officially discriminate in many ways, this is not surprising.[8] Nonetheless, the Census data allow us to describe a large sample of gay and lesbian families. Same-sex couple households were reported in 99.3% of all U.S. counties and represented every ethnic, racial, income, and adult age group.[9] These same-sex couple families were about as racially diverse as the overall U.S. population.[10]

Same-sex couple households were reported in 99.3% of all U.S. counties, and represented every ethnic, racial, income, and adult age group.

PARENTING AMONG SAME-SEX COUPLES AND SINGLE GAY PARENTS

Many same-sex couples are raising children. Estimates of the number of lesbian or gay parents in the U.S. range

Data from the 2000 Census indicate that 34% of lesbian couples and 22% of gay male couples have at least one child under 18 years of age living in their home.

from two to eight million.[11] These figures include many single parents who are lesbian, gay, or bisexual. Data from the 2000 Census indicate that 34% of lesbian couples and 22% of gay male couples have at least one child under 18 years of age living in their home.[12] While these figures may not seem that high, when compared with parenting rates among married heterosexual couples (46% of whom are raising children), lesbian couples on the 2000 Census parent at about three-quarters the rate of married straight couples, and gay male couples parent at about half the rate as married straight couples. Many more are parents of children who do not live with them, or are "empty nesters" because their children are away at college or living on their own as adults.

The states with the highest prevalence of parenting among same-sex couple households on the 2000 Census were Southern and rural states. For example, in Mississippi 31% of gay male couples who self-identified on the Census were raising children, as were 44% of lesbian couples. This compares with 22% of gay male couples and 34% of lesbian couples nationally. South Dakota and Alaska also reported high rates of parenting by same-sex couples. Southern states reported parenting among an average of 24% of gay male couples and 36% of lesbian couples, both figures two percentage points above the national average.[13]

The vast majority of children's advocacy organizations, including the American Academy of Pediatrics,[14] the National Association of Social Workers,[15] and the American Psychological Association (APA),[16] recognize that gay and lesbian parents are just as good as heterosexual parents, and that children thrive in gay- and lesbian-headed families. One APA publication reports, "not a single study has found children of gay or lesbian parents to be disadvantaged in any significant respect relative to children of heterosexual parents."[17] Other peer-reviewed social science

Density of Same-Sex Couples
vs. all coupled households

Source: U.S. Census Bureau (2003).
Married-couple and unmarried-partner households: 2000.
http://www.census.gov/prod/2003pubs/censr-5.pdf.

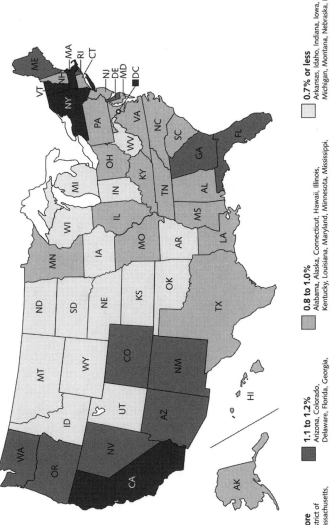

1.3% or more
California, District of
Columbia, Massachusetts,
New York, Vermont

1.1 to 1.2%
Arizona, Colorado,
Delaware, Florida, Georgia,
Maine, Nevada, New Mexico,
Oregon, Rhode Island,
Washington

0.8 to 1.0%
Alabama, Alaska, Connecticut, Hawaii, Illinois,
Kentucky, Louisiana, Maryland, Minnesota, Mississippi,
Missouri, New Hampshire, New Jersey, North Carolina,
Ohio, Pennsylvania, South Carolina, Tennessee, Texas,
Virginia, Puerto Rico

0.7% or less
Arkansas, Idaho, Indiana, Iowa, Kansas,
Michigan, Montana, Nebraska, North Dakota,
Oklahoma, South Dakota, Utah,
West Virginia, Wisconsin, Wyoming

research has also found that children being raised by gay, lesbian, and bisexual parents are not disadvantaged relative to their peers raised by heterosexual parents.[18]

Race and Parenting

Some studies indicate a significant prevalence of parenting among lesbian and gay African Americans and other people of color. The National Gay and Lesbian Task Force's 2000 Black Pride Survey queried nearly 2,700 African American gay, lesbian, bisexual, and transgender people in nine cities. It found that nearly 40% of black lesbians and bisexual women, 15% of black gay and bisexual men, and 15% of black transgender people reported having children. Twenty-five percent of the women surveyed at Black Gay Pride celebrations, and 4% of the men, reported that those children lived with them.[19] The 2000 U.S. Census data indicate that black lesbian couples are raising children at nearly the same rate as black married heterosexual couples. Black same-sex couples parent at nearly twice the rate as white same-sex couples.[20]

Anti-gay parenting policies may disproportionately affect gay, lesbian, and bisexual people of color.

The 1990 Census data—reflecting the first time the U.S. Census allowed cohabiting gay couples to self-identify—indicate that ethnic minority women in same-sex relationships may be more likely than white, non-Hispanic lesbians to have children.[21] These statistics indicate that anti-gay parenting policies and laws may disproportionately affect gay, lesbian, and bisexual people of color.

Income and Parenting

Despite the widespread stereotype that gay men and lesbians are wealthier than the general population, as many anti-gay groups claim, research shows otherwise.[22] An analysis of 1990 Census data and U.S. General Social Survey data from the late 1980s and early

Concentration of Same-Sex Couples: Missouri

Source: Bradford, J., Barrett, K., and Honnold, J. A. (2002). *The 2000 Census and Same-Sex Households: A User's Guide.* New York: The National Gay and Lesbian Task Force Policy Institute, the Survey and Evaluation Research Laboratory, and The Fenway Institute.

2000
Total Same-Sex Households: 9,428 (436% increase)

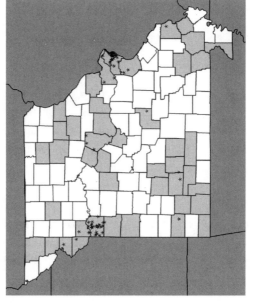

1990
Total Same-Sex Households: 1,931

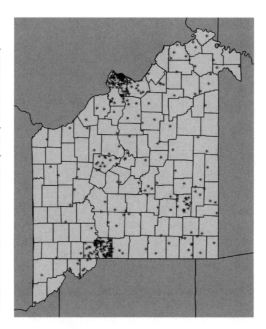

* = 25 same-sex households

counties reporting one or more same-sex households

counties reporting zero same-sex households

Atlanta, GA

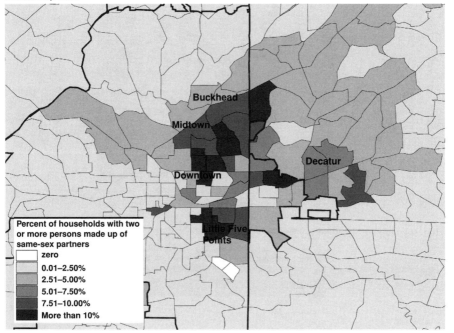

Map by Ivan Cheung, Ph.D.

1990s indicates that gay men earn about one-fifth to one-quarter less than their heterosexual counterparts. Lesbians appear to earn about the same as heterosexual women, but lesbian couples earn less than straight couples because women, on average, earn less than men.[23] Preliminary data from the 2000 Census indicate similar earnings between same-sex couple households and opposite-sex couple households.[24]

Preliminary data from the 2000 Census indicate similar earnings between same-sex couple households and opposite-sex couple households.

Low- and moderate-income gay families confront many obstacles. They also face additional challenges because many public policies and private employers refuse to accept their identities or recognize their families. Poor lesbians and gay men grapple with a welfare system that increasingly favors married heterosexual couples over single parents and all unmarried couples, including same-sex couples.[25] Homeless same-sex couples may be unable to apply for public housing as a family. The lack of equal access to marriage and adoption forces many gay couples to spend thousands of dollars on legal documents to protect their families—documents that are not always upheld in court or respected by hospitals, banks, and other institutions. Those who cannot afford such legal fees can find their families without even minimal protections in times of crisis. Gay individuals and families in need of social services may experience hostility, discrimination, and even proselytizing at the hands of social service providers under the faith-based initiative.[26]

CUSTODY RIGHTS

When a Parent Comes Out

Some lesbian, gay, and bisexual parents discover or come to terms with their sexual orientation while they are married to someone of the opposite sex. When these marriages end, parents are often confronted with custody challenges. In nearly every state, custody decisions must be determined according to the "best interests of the child." Even so, application of this general rule varies greatly from state to state, and even from judge to judge. The District of Columbia is currently the only jurisdiction in the country that has a statute explicitly guaranteeing that sexual orientation cannot, in and of itself, be a conclusive factor in determining custody or visitation,[27] although courts in several states have ruled as such.[28]

However, in Tennessee in 2002, a gay father was jailed for two days for revealing his sexual orientation to his son.[29] Also that year, Alabama Chief Justice Roy Moore denied a lesbian mother custody of her children based on the criminalization of homosexuality under the state's sodomy law. Moore wrote in justifying his decision to deny the mother custody, "Common law designates

In Tennessee in 2002, a gay father was jailed for two days for revealing his sexual orientation to his son.

homosexuality as an inherent evil, and if a person openly engages in such a practice, that fact alone would render him or her an unfit parent."[30]

When Gay Parents Split Up

Due to the current ban on marriage for same-sex couples, gay relationships are by definition cohabiting relationships. In this sense, then, noncohabitation requirements discriminate against gay and lesbian parents.[31] In order to be able to maintain visitation rights in some parts of the country, the noncustodial parent is prohibited from living with an unmarried partner.[32] There have been numerous cases in which nonbiological parents are left without visitation or custody rights when their relationships end. Supreme courts in six states have found that nonbiological parents do have the legal right to seek visitation and/or custody of the children they raise, but only if they meet specified standards.[33] In 1999, in an effort to prevent court litigation, several gay organizations and individuals authored a set of ethical standards for child-custody disputes in same-sex relationships.[34]

ADOPTION RIGHTS

Gay and lesbian adults are among the thousands who adopt children each year. Some adopt children they are raising with a partner (often the biological child of their partner), thereby creating a legal bond where a familial one already exists. Some are chosen by family members or close friends to adopt a child upon the death or incapacitation of the child's own parents. Many adopt through public or private agencies, domestically and internationally. Some work through intermediaries to identify women wishing to have their babies adopted and to reach agreements directly with those birth mothers.

Anti-Gay Adoption Laws and Regulations

Most U.S. states permit adoptions by single individuals, including gay men and lesbians. However, a few states explicitly prohibit or regularly deny adoptions by gay people. Many states deny lesbian and gay couples the ability to jointly adopt a child, or for one parent to adopt a child that already has a legal bond to the other parent. In contrast, married couples are free to pursue joint adoption, and stepparent adoption by a spouse tends to be a simple process.

Six states limit the right of gay men, lesbians, or same-sex couples to adopt or foster parent.[35] Due in part to Anita Bryant's "Save Our Children" campaign that overthrew Miami-Dade County's sexual orientation nondiscrimination law in 1977, Florida has explicitly banned adoptions by "homosexuals" for more than a quarter century. Utah prohibits adoption by "cohabiting" unmarried couples, which applies to gay couples in Utah and 48 other states. Mississippi bans "same-sex couples" from adopting. While Arkansas does not prohibit gays from adopting, since 1999 its Child Welfare Agency Review Board has banned gays and lesbians from foster parenting. In spring 2003, North Dakota passed a law targeting gay adoption that allows agencies that receive state contracts and licenses to refuse to place children with prospective parents whom they object to on religious grounds. Oklahoma passed an anti-gay adoption law in May 2004. In other states where lesbians and gay men are technically able to adopt as individuals, judges sometimes intervene to prevent the placement of a child with a lesbian or gay parent.

Six states limit the right of gay men, lesbians, or same-sex couples to adopt or foster parent.

Joint and Second-Parent Adoption

Adoptions that codify the parental relationship of both parents are essential to ensuring the rights and security of children of same-sex couple parents. When a child is not biologically related to either parent, a joint adoption allows both parents to simultaneously adopt a child. During

Anti-Gay Parenting Laws in the U.S.
(As of June 2004)

Source: National Gay & Lesbian Task Force, 2004.

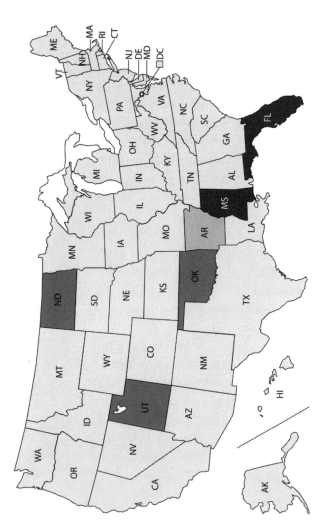

Laws prohibiting adoption
Florida (prohibits adoption by "homosexuals");
Mississippi (prohibits same-sex couples from adopting)

Laws restricting adoptions and foster care placement
Utah (prohibits adoption by a person who is cohabiting—defined as residing with another person and being involved in a sexual relationship with that person—in a relationship that is not legally valid); North Dakota (allows adoption agencies to discriminate against prospective gay parents and others based on religious objection); Oklahoma (prohibits the recognition of an adoption by more than one individual of the same sex from any other state or foreign jurisdiction).

Regulations or policies prohibiting or restricting adoption and/or foster care
Arkansas (administrative rule prohibiting gay men and lesbians from being foster parents)

the 1980s, lower courts in the San Francisco Bay Area began granting lesbian and gay couples the right to adopt children jointly and simultaneously. Since then, courts have been allowing such adoptions more frequently. Joint adoption is currently available in the District of Columbia, California, Connecticut, Massachusetts, New Jersey, New York, and Vermont and has been granted at the trial court level in other jurisdictions.[36]

A second-parent adoption allows the biological or adoptive parent to retain his or her parental rights, while consenting to the adoption of the child by his or her partner. Second-parent adoptions have been in use since 1985, when Alaska granted one of the first to a same-sex couple. Since the mid-1980s, courts in nearly two dozen states have approved second-parent adoptions.[37] In 2000, the Connecticut legislature created a mechanism for joint and second-parent adoptions.[38] Second-parent adoptions are generally possible only when a third party does not already have legal parental rights. While courts in 20 states have permitted second-parent adoptions by gay partners, and laws in three states explicitly permit second-parent adoption by a gay partner, children of same-sex couples in most states still live with the economic and emotional insecurity of not having their relationship with their second mother or father recognized. In four states, courts have ruled that the state's adoption law does not allow for second-parent or stepparent adoption by gay partners.[39]

Without the legal protections that come with adoption, a child can be left without access to basic benefits, including health insurance and inheritance rights. If the legally recognized parent dies, a child may be removed from the custody of his or her other parent, unless that parent has been designated the child's guardian in a will. If a child of gay parents becomes sick, the legal parent's partner may be unable to authorize medical treatment, and may even be denied hospital visitation rights.

Joint adoption is currently available in the District of Columbia, California, Connecticut, Massachusetts, New Jersey, New York, and Vermont.

ELDER COUPLES

Gay and lesbian elders experience a number of particular concerns as they age. In a recent study, three in four gay elders reported not being completely open about their sexual orientation to health-care workers.[40] Discrimination following disclosure of sexual orientation has been reported in nursing homes and senior centers.[41] Social Security and retirement plan regulations deny gay elders access to funds from systems they pay into throughout their working lives, but cannot access due to the unequal treatment of same-sex couples.

Social Security and Pensions

Nearly two-thirds of U.S. retirees rely on Social Security for more than half of their annual income; for 15% of seniors, Social Security is their only source of income.[42] Social Security survivor benefits allow widows, widowers, and dependent children to put food on the table, and fairly compensate them when their spouse pays into the system his or her whole life but dies before being able to enjoy these retirement savings. But gay and lesbian survivors are not eligible for these benefits, although they have paid the same taxes. The September 11 attacks illustrated the unfairness of this policy: same-sex survivors of victims were denied survivor benefits as well as funds from the victims compensation fund administered by the U.S. Justice Department. Gay partners are also ineligible for spousal benefits, which allow a partner to earn about half his or her life partner's Social Security payment if that rate is higher.

The Retirement Equity Act of 1984 created spousal rights to a worker's pension benefits while both are living and after the worker's death. Though such rights can be waived, the measure was intended to protect widows or widowers from a severe loss of income. The gay or lesbian partner of a pension plan participant cannot claim such rights. When a retired worker dies, gay or straight, the re-

The Cost of Unequal Treatment under Social Security[43]

Thorsten Behrens, 33, and Christopher Schiebel, 32, have been in a committed relationship for five years. They live in western Massachusetts. Thorsten has no children, but Christopher has two children from a previous marriage that they are both raising. Thorsten is the main breadwinner. In 2002, Thorsten earned a total of $44,198, and Christopher earned $4,044 in W-2 reported income and $3,645 in unemployment compensation.

Spousal benefit: Based on their current earnings, upon retirement Thorsten and Christopher's combined monthly Social Security retirement benefit would be $1,830—representing $303 per month for Christopher and $1,527 per month for Thorsten. However, if they could marry and their marriage were recognized by the Social Security Administration, Christopher would be eligible for the spousal benefit, which would allow him to earn half of Thorsten's monthly payment, or an additional $461 per month. Their combined Social Security retirement benefit would be $2,291 per month, almost 25% more than they would otherwise receive.

Survivor benefit: If Thorsten and Christopher were able to legally marry, and then Thorsten died, Christopher would be eligible for the survivor benefit upon retirement. This would mean he would receive $1,527 per month from Social Security instead of the $303 he would otherwise receive. If Thorsten and Christopher could marry and then Thorsten died, Christopher would receive $1,224 (more than 400%) more in Social Security benefits in retirement.

maining pension wealth can be distributed to any benefi-ciary. But certain tax rollover treatment for these distri-butions—a significant advantage—is available only to a spouse.

If a person dies after becoming vested in a pension plan, but before reaching retirement age, a spouse is enti-tled to begin receiving benefits the year that the deceased would have started drawing on the pension. Or the spouse can take a lump-sum distribution and roll the full amount over into an individual retirement account

COMBINED MONTHLY SOCIAL SECURITY RETIREMENT BENEFIT
for Thorsten and Christopher's family

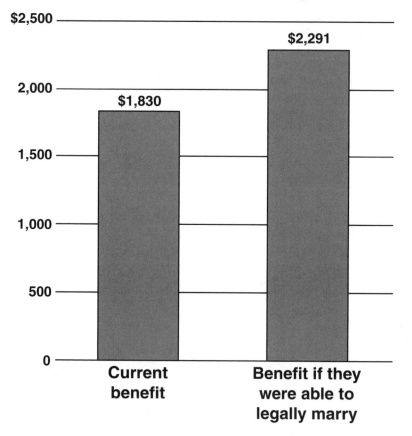

Upon retirement, Thorsten and Christopher's combined monthly Social Security retirement benefit would be 25% higher if they were legally married.

Source: National Gay and Lesbian Task Force Policy Institute

(IRA), where it maintains its tax-deferred status. A surviving same-sex partner can be a named beneficiary of the pension upon the participant's death, but the proceeds are not tax-favored. If someone with a 401(k) plan dies and the beneficiary is a married spouse, then he or she may roll over the total amount of the distribution into an IRA without paying income tax. But if the surviving beneficiary is a same-sex partner, the pension distribution is subject to a 20% federal withholding tax.[44]

Strong majorities of Americans support treating same-sex couples equally under Social Security policy (68%) and laws governing inheritance (73%).[45] In January 2002, the Democratic National Committee called for equal treatment of gay and lesbian couples by the Social Security Administration. All the Democratic candidates for president in 2004 supported equal treatment of gay partners under Social Security except Senator Joseph Lieberman, who said he was studying the issue.

68% of Americans support treating same-sex couples equally under Social Security policy. 73% of Americans support giving same-sex couples equal inheritance rights.

Medicaid Spend-Down

Other senior family issues include the Medicaid spend-down provision. Following the death of a spouse in a nursing home or assisted care facility, Medicaid regulations allow the surviving widow or widower of a married heterosexual couple to remain in the couple's home for the rest of his or her life without jeopardizing the right to Medicaid coverage. Upon the survivor's death, the state may then take the home to recoup the costs of terminal care. Because same-sex couples cannot marry, they may be forced to choose between their home and life's savings or medical coverage.[46]

HEALTH CARE

In times of illness, most people rely on the support of their families. Hospitals routinely call on an incapacitated patient's next of kin to make medical decisions. Many people receive their health insurance through family members. But because they are not recognized as legitimate families, gay and lesbian couples face unique problems when dealing with the health-care system.

Health care–related rights available exclusively to married partners include:

- Important hospital visitation rights.
- The right to make medical, legal, and financial decisions for an incapacitated partner.
- The right to take time from work to care for an ill partner
- Access to health insurance for one's partner and one's partner's children.
- The right to make funeral arrangements for a deceased partner.
- The right to sue for wrongful death, in most jurisdictions.
- The right to domestic violence protection from an abusive partner, in three states: Delaware, Montana, and South Carolina.[47]

If a gay man or lesbian is incapacitated in the hospital, his or her closest blood relative will automatically be given the power to make decisions about care unless a medical power of attorney form has been completed. If this form exists, then the specified health-care proxy may act on behalf of the incapacitated person and make decisions as his or her agent. But even if armed with a durable power of attorney, a health-care proxy, or other legally binding documents, gay couples' familial rights are still sometimes unacknowledged by hospital staff.[48]

Family and Medical Leave

The Family and Medical Leave Act, a federal law passed in 1993, provides up to 12 weeks of unpaid leave after the birth or adoption of a child, to facilitate recovery from a "serious health condition," or to care for an immediate family member who is extremely sick. But "family" is defined specifically as being headed by heterosexual couples or single parents, and excludes those headed by gay men or lesbians, thus preventing them from taking care of their families on equal terms with their heterosexual counterparts, and exposing them to additional vulnerability in the workplace.[49]

California is the only state that provides paid family leave to employees. It allows state residents to take six weeks of paid leave from work to care for an ill relative—including a domestic partner—or after the birth, adoption, or foster placement of a child. While on leave, most workers are paid at a rate of about 55% of their salary. This is funded by a payroll tax that averages $26 per year per employee.[50] Two other states, Hawaii and Vermont, provide unpaid family leave for same-sex partners as well as married spouses. Nearly two dozen other states provide some form of unpaid family and medical leave, but to spouses only, not same-sex partners.

UNEQUAL TAX TREATMENT OF SAME-SEX COUPLES

Another area where gay people face discrimination is in tax laws. Same-sex couples confront significantly different tax burdens than do married couples. Specifically, same-sex couples cannot benefit from the tax exemptions married couples can claim with regard to gift taxes and estate taxes. Moreover, gay and lesbian partners are liable for taxes on any domestic partner benefits they receive. Finally, gay men and lesbians face obstacles in claiming their partners as dependents. There are three main areas of tax disparity of particular concern:

Same-sex couples cannot benefit from the tax exemptions married couples can claim with regard to gift taxes and estate taxes.

1. Married spouses can transfer an unlimited amount of money to each other without incurring taxes—unless either spouse is not a U.S. citizen, under which circumstances they can transfer up to $101,000 per year without

being liable for gift tax. The IRS stipulates, however, that a person who transfers more than $11,000 to someone who is not his or her spouse is liable to pay a gift tax on the amount that exceeds $11,000, unless it is designated to pay for tuition or medical expenses.

2. Whereas gift taxes apply to monetary transfers between unmarried people while they are alive, estate tax applies to monetary transfers between unmarried people in the event that one of them dies. While spouses can inherit each other's estates tax free, for unmarried couples the value of the estate exceeding $675,000— or, after 2006, $1 million—will be taxed.

3. Most employees enjoy, tax-free, the health insurance they and their spouse or dependents receive from their employer.[51] Same-sex couples, however, do not qualify as spouses and normally do not qualify as dependents.[52] The value of their domestic partner benefits, such as health insurance, is taxable income, paid by the employee. This can have significant tax consequences, even to the point of making it financially detrimental for an unmarried partner to access health benefits. For example, if the value of the health benefits is enough to bump an employee up to the next tax bracket, then they could pay more for their partner's benefits than if they acquired insurance independently.

Even in many "gay-friendly" communities, same-sex couples can assemble only a patchwork of rights that does not approach the range of rights and protections granted to married heterosexual couples and their children. Although civil unions and domestic partnership policies are welcome developments, only full access to the institution of civil marriage affords equality under federal law, including Social Security, immigration policy, federal tax law, and other important policy frameworks.

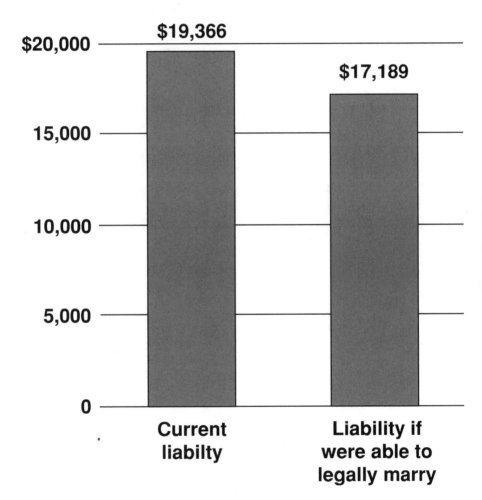

TOTAL INCOME TAX LIABILITY (2002) for Donna T. and Donna M.

- $20,000 — $19,366
- $17,189
- 15,000
- 10,000
- 5,000
- 0

Current liabilty

Liability if were able to legally marry

The Cost of Unequal Treatment
under Federal and State Taxes[53]

Donna Triggs and Donna Moore are both 54 years old and live in Massachusetts. They met in college 36 years ago, have been in a relationship for seven years, and rent a home together. They each have two children from previous marriages, all four of whom are adults. A medical technologist, Donna T. had an annual income of about $72,000 in 2002. Donna M., a massage therapist, earned about $25,000 in 2002. Donna M. is covered under Donna T.'s employer domestic partner health insurance.

Because in 2002 they were unable to legally marry, Donna T. and Donna M. are considered single persons in Massachusetts and by the Internal Revenue Service (IRS). Their combined federal and state income tax liability in 2002 was $19,366. If they were able to file a joint federal and state income tax return as a married couple, Donna T. and Donna M. would incur a total federal and state income tax liability of only $17,189. Because they could not legally marry and because their marriage would not be recognized by the IRS, Donna Triggs and Donna Moore paid $2,177 (13%) more in taxes in 2002 than they would have if they could marry and file joint returns.

4

Gay Rights on the Political Stage

THE FIRST WAVE OF ANTI-GAY BALLOT CAMPAIGNS

For three decades, the national anti-gay movement—composed of politically conservative, religiously and ideologically motivated activist groups—has used anti-gay ballot questions at the local and state level as "its central strategy" in opposing legal equality for lesbian, gay, and bisexual people.[1] In the past few years it has sought the repeal of gender identity nondiscrimination laws—laws that protect transgender[2] people against discrimination—as well as laws banning discrimination on the basis of sexual orientation. Anti-gay activists, sometimes local but usually receiving a great deal of support from the national anti-gay movement, have launched more than 100 anti-gay ballot initiatives and referenda since the first anti-gay ballot campaign was launched in Boulder, Colorado, in 1974.[3] This referendum repealed a sexual orientation nondiscrimination ordinance. Anita Bryant's successful "Save Our Children" campaign, which repealed Miami-Dade County, Florida's sexual orientation nondiscrimination law in 1977, was the second anti-gay ballot measure but the

Referenda are popular votes on a law passed by a legislature or under consideration by a legislature. 24 states allow citizens to demand a referendum through the petition process.

Initiatives **are laws proposed directly by voters that require only a minimum number of signatures to get on the ballot. 23 states allow initiatives.**

first to reach national prominence. Following Bryant's more than two-to-one victory, five anti-gay ballot questions ensued across the U.S. in 1978, three on the West Coast and two in the Midwest. The wave of anti-gay measures continued into the 1980s. Most were successful and resulted in the repeal of sexual orientation nondiscrimination laws.

1972–1980: THE EMERGENCE OF GAY ISSUES IN PRESIDENTIAL POLITICS

Even as the gay and lesbian community struggled to resist the increasing number of anti-gay ballot campaigns spreading across the country, activists also sought support for legal equality from Democratic Party leaders. Gay rights language was proposed for the 1972 Democratic Party platform. Partly to court California gay activists, Senator George McGovern issued "a seven-point gay rights plank that satisfied virtually every demand the fledgling gay movement was making."[4] However, after becoming the presumed nominee, McGovern had second thoughts and lobbied against adding pro-gay language to the party platform. Such language would not be adopted until 1980. Still, the 1972 Democratic Convention made history when one of only two openly gay delegates, San Francisco activist Jim Foster, spoke about gay rights before the crowd.[5] As gay activist groups, community-based organizations, and Democratic clubs proliferated, Democratic politicians increasingly spoke in favor of sexual orientation nondiscrimination laws. Georgia Governor Jimmy Carter did so when running for president, but then failed to issue an executive order or promote the federal gay rights bill once he was elected. According to one lesbian activist involved in negotiations with the Democratic Party leadership in the mid-1970s, she and other gay activists were told they "were an embarrassment" to Carter.

The 1980 presidential campaign was the first in which gay rights were directly addressed by presidential candidates or party platforms. Senator Ted Kennedy's challenge to President Carter garnered significant gay and lesbian support. Kennedy returned the favor by helping insert pro–gay rights language into the Democratic Party platform for the first time. The Republicans adopted coded anti-gay platform language (traditional family values) in 1980, setting a pattern of polarization that continues a quarter-century later. GOP candidates Ronald Reagan, George Bush, and John Connolly made anti-gay statements. And, as Urvashi Vaid notes,

> Even Bush's 1988 Willie Horton ads had an anti-gay ancestry: during the 1980 campaign, a Republican ad featured a montage from the San Francisco Freedom Day Parade, with an ominous voice-over: "The gays in San Francisco elected a mayor." As the picture faded into a still shot of President Carter, the voice-over prophesied, "Now they're going to elect a President."[6]

Gay rights was a central issue in the 1980 presidential race, at least in some parts of the country. A back cover, full-page ad for Ronald Reagan in the October 23, 1980, *South Boston Marshall* urged voters, "Don't let the *Boston Globe* make up your mind. The liberal newspapers are in bed with Carter and his 'progressive' record on busing, gay rights, affirmative action and prayer in the public schools." Anyone familiar with the history of South Boston, a bastion of white resistance to school desegregation and busing, knows that to list gay rights between busing and affirmative action indicates how important this issue was to conservatives there. A chart in the ad lists Reagan's and Carter's positions on eight "issues of importance to our community." On the sixth issue, gay rights, Reagan "opposes special treatment," while Carter "supports it."[7] Reagan won Massachusetts, which usually votes Democratic, in 1980 and 1984.

With multimillion-dollar budgets and cutting-edge technology, national organizations increased the sophistication and effectiveness of anti-gay activism throughout the 1980s.

THE REAGAN YEARS

At least 15 large national organizations with multi-million-dollar budgets and cutting-edge computer and direct-mail technology made anti-gay activism in the 1980s more effective and sophisticated than the moral crusades of Anita Bryant and her colleagues in the 1970s.[8] Conservative evangelical preachers also promoted right wing political causes through new televised religious programs. Reagan appointed Focus on the Family's Gary Bauer (later to lead the Family Research Council, a spin-off of Focus on the Family) as a domestic policy advisor, and Reagan supported the Family Protection Act, which would have banned federal funds to "any organization that suggests that homosexuality can be an acceptable alternative lifestyle."[9] When AIDS emerged in the United States, first within the gay male community, where it was initially known as Gay Related Immune Deficiency, anti-gay activists argued that homosexuality inevitably led to disease and death. In the 1980s, anti-gay groups portrayed homosexuality as a gay disease or, as some called it, "the gay plague."[10] The Moral Majority's Jerry Falwell, commentator Pat Buchanan, and others portrayed AIDS as "God's retribution" for sodomy. Televangelist Pat Robertson referred to AIDS as "God's way of weeding his garden."[11] In a 1987 fundraising letter, Falwell accused gay men of deliberately poisoning the nation's blood supply, because "they know they are going to die—and they are going to take as many people with them as they can."[12] The American Red Cross, however, had already implemented a ban on male homosexual donations of blood. And lesbians—female homosexuals—were and still are at lower risk for HIV and AIDS than heterosexual women and men in the U.S. In Africa and the rest of the developing world, HIV is primarily spread through heterosexual sex, intravenous drug use, and poor health-care practices.

Political attacks on people with AIDS often took frightening forms. In 1986 and 1988, Californians voted on whether to quarantine people with AIDS. These ballot questions, sponsored by Lyndon LaRouche, were rejected.[13] Rev. Lou Sheldon, former director of the Briggs Initiative and now head of the Traditional Values Coalition, supported the AIDS quarantine propositions.[14]

Even when, after years of delay, hostility, and inaction, the federal government finally provided funds for AIDS prevention and treatment, a 1987 amendment sponsored by Senator Jesse Helms (R-NC) and attached to many funding bills in the late 1980s and early 1990s banned the use of federal funds for AIDS education that "promotes or encourages homosexual behavior." This had a chilling effect on attempts to teach sexually active youth and adults how to avoid sexually transmitted diseases and unwanted pregnancy. It was particularly harmful to efforts to stem the spread of HIV among gay and bisexual men, who in the 1980s were the crucible of the epidemic in the United States. Helms-inspired "no promo homo" laws were also passed in states across the country, inhibiting effective AIDS prevention and interfering with efforts to stop school-based harassment and violence against gay, lesbian, and bisexual students.

The Republican Party continued to oppose legal equality for gay men and lesbians. In a 1984 *Presidential Biblical Scorecard*, President Reagan criticized gay couple families and vowed to "resist the efforts of some to obtain government endorsement of homosexuality."[15] The 1984 Democratic ticket largely ignored gay issues, and the 1988 candidate, Massachusetts Governor Michael Dukakis, was hostile to gay rights, having endorsed a ban on gay foster parents in 1985.[16]

LATE 1980s AND EARLY 1990s: THE RISE IN ANTI-GAY ACTIVISM

In the late 1980s and early 1990s, there was a dramatic increase in anti-gay activism, particularly through the medium of ballot campaigns, which became "a centerpiece

Anti-gay groups put forward African American spokespeople to argue that gay rights threaten the civil rights of people of color.

of [the] activist program" of the religious right.[17] Many of these ballot campaigns sought to repeal or prevent gay rights laws at the local and state level. Most passed, especially those that were local (as opposed to statewide) and those that involved repealing a nondiscrimination law or pro-gay policy or program.[18] Initiatives aimed at preempting gay rights provisions were less likely to succeed.[19] Notable exceptions were the initiatives banning sexual orientation nondiscrimination laws in Colorado and Cincinnati, Ohio.

The "No Special Rights" and "Legitimate Minorities" Claims

What was different about this second, larger wave of anti-gay ballot campaigns was the more explicit deployment of a central, unifying theme: that homosexuality is an individual choice, not a condition or status, and therefore different from race and undeserving of legal protection.[20] Gay rights were portrayed as "special rights" and as a threat to the civil rights of "legitimate minorities," such as African Americans and other racial minorities. Anti-gay groups increasingly put forward African American spokespeople to argue that gay rights threaten the civil rights of people of color, as the Traditional Values Coalition did in its 1992 video *Gay Rights, Special Rights.* Civil rights struggles were presented as a zero-sum game between blacks (presumed to be straight) and gays (presumed to be white). If gays get civil rights, the video argued, this will mean fewer rights for African Americans.

Gay rights continue to be characterized as special rights. Arguments such as these often portray gay people as privileged playboys who do not need civil rights protections. Proponents of this view cite statistics derived from reader surveys conducted by gay newspapers and magazines that claim gays are disproportionately wealthy and therefore undeserving of nondiscrimination protections. They claim that gays have a higher average income than "average American[s]" and particularly African Americans.[21] In fact, research indicates that gay men earn roughly 20% to 25% less than their heterosexual counterparts. Lesbians appear to earn about the same as heterosexual women, but lesbian couples earn less than straight couples because women, on average, earn less than men.[22]

As Suzanne Goldberg notes, the concept of "special rights" is legally meaningless: "no such 'rights' exist."[23] In other words, anti-gay groups have won dozens of anti-gay ballot campaigns based on claims that are patently false. Anti-gay groups define "special rights" to include minority status, affirmative action, quotas, and special class status. Scott Nakagawa notes that anti-gay groups contend that gays are not eligible for "minority status and all the privileges thereof." This promotes another right wing myth that being a member of a racial minority group provides one with privileges.[24] In fact, racial, gender, religion, and sexual orientation nondiscrimination laws protect everyone against discrimination on the basis of their race, sex, religion, or sexual orientation, not just members of demographic minorities or women. In the process of allegedly protecting (presumably all straight) people of color against the alleged threat posed by (presumably all white) gay people, anti-gay activists reinforce misconceptions about nondiscrimination laws, affirmative action, and minority status that, in fact, hurt people of color.[25] Sexual orientation nondiscrimination laws do not promote affirmative action or hiring quotas for gay people.

The view that sexual orientation nondiscrimination laws represent "special rights" is shared by President George W. Bush as well as many other conservative politicians. During the second presidential debate in October 2000, when asked if "gays and lesbians should have the

Research indicates that gay men earn roughly 20% to 25% less than their heterosexual counterparts. Lesbians appear to earn the same as heterosexual women, but lesbian couples earn less than straight couples because women, on average, earn less than men.

Sexual orientation nondiscrimination laws do not promote affirmative action or hiring quotas for gay people.

same rights as other Americans," Bush responded, "Yes. I don't think they ought to have special rights. But I think they ought to have the same rights." When asked to elaborate on what he meant by "special rights," Bush responded, "Well, it'd be if they're given special protective status."[26] White House spokesman Ari Fleischer reiterated this claim in April 2003: "The President has always said that when it comes to legal matters, that it's a question of different groups, homosexual groups, gay groups should not have special rights or special privileges."[27]

Most anti-gay ballot questions in the 1980s and early 1990s targeted sexual orientation nondiscrimination laws, efforts to combat anti-gay harassment in schools, and sex education. The first ballot question to target same-sex marriage was a 1994 anti-gay initiative in Idaho, which was rejected by a 1% margin, or 3,000 votes. Idaho's Proposition One would have prevented the state from granting "minority status" or affirmative action to homosexuals, and explicitly allowed state agencies to consider "private sexual behaviors" in employment decisions. It also forbade state recognition of marriages or domestic partnerships of same-sex couples. Finally, Proposition One prohibited the promotion of homosexuality in schools, including in library books.[28]

In 1996, in *Romer v. Evans*, the U.S. Supreme Court struck down Colorado's Amendment 2, passed in 1992, which banned sexual orientation nondiscrimination laws in that state. The Court ruled that Amendment 2 violated the U.S. Constitution's guarantee of equal protection of the laws, and that it was motivated not by any rational state interest but solely by "animus" toward gay, lesbian, and bisexual people.[29] Despite this ruling, the U.S. Supreme Court declined to review a federal court's ruling upholding Cincinnati's law, which was modeled after the Colorado measure. Cincinnati's anti-gay provision was finally repealed by voters in November 2004. More narrow ballot measures repealing existing nondiscrimination laws have continued to pass in Maine (locally in 1995, and statewide in 1998 and 2000) and several municipalities around the country.

PRO-GAY ADVANCES IN THE 1990s

The 1990s were a decade in which gay issues emerged onto the national political scene in unprecedented ways. The policy outcomes of the debates over gays in the military and same-sex marriage represented significant setbacks for those seeking equality. Aside from President Clinton's 1998 executive order banning sexual orientation discrimination in the federal civilian workforce, there were few tangible political gains at the federal level, due in part to Congressional inaction on employment discrimination and hate crimes. But despite minimal progress and even retrenchment at the level of national policy, the 1990s witnessed three developments that strengthened the movement for gay equality overall: the dramatic growth in local and state nondiscrimination laws and partner recognition policies; the emergence of majority support for legal equality in all areas except marriage/partner recognition and parenting; and the emergence of a sizable, discrete gay voting bloc.

The Growth of Nondiscrimination and Family Recognition Policies

In 1990, less than 20 million Americans, or about 10% of the population, lived in a jurisdiction with a gay rights law. As of 2004, some 128 million Americans, or 45% of the population, live in a city, county, or state that outlaws sexual orientation discrimination. Fourteen states have sexual orientation nondiscrimination laws. Today, nearly 70 million Americans, or 24% of the population, live in a municipality or state with a gender identity

As of early 2004, some 128 million Americans, or 45% of the population, live in a city, county, or state that outlaws sexual orientation discrimination.

nondiscrimination law; in 1990, little more than 1 million Americans lived in three cities with such laws.[30] Four states have gender identity nondiscrimination laws.[31] In an additional nine states, executive orders protect public sector employees against sexual orientation discrimination, and two states have similar executive orders that also include gender identity.[32]

A similar expansion in partner benefits occurred over the past decade or so, with a dozen states and hundreds of municipalities offering registries to same-sex couples and benefits to the partners of public sector employees.[33] The private sector has also adopted nondiscrimination and partner recognition policies; a majority of Fortune 500 companies now offer domestic partner benefits to same-sex partners of their workers.[34] This expansion of nondiscrimination and family recognition policies results from the hard work of thousands of grassroots activists, but also from the increased support of the general public for such laws. However, federal nondiscrimination legislation, first introduced into Congress in 1975 by Congresswoman Bella Abzug of New York, has not yet passed Congress.

Growth in Public Opinion Support for Gay Equality

Over the past decade, strong majorities have emerged in public opinion polls in support of the right to serve in the military,[35] employment nondiscrimination laws, and equal benefits for same-sex partners.[36] In the 2000 National Election Study, 56% of Republican voters, 70% of Independents, and 75% of Democrats supported sexual orientation nondiscrimination laws.[37] Nearly nine in ten Americans support the principle of sexual orientation nondiscrimination, if not the laws required to enforce this practice.[38] Nearly all American parents support sex education to prevent unwanted pregnancy and sexually transmitted diseases.[39]

Nondiscrimination Laws in the U.S.

Inclusive of Sexual Orientation and Gender Identity (as of April 2004)

Source: National Gay & Lesbian Task Force, 2004.

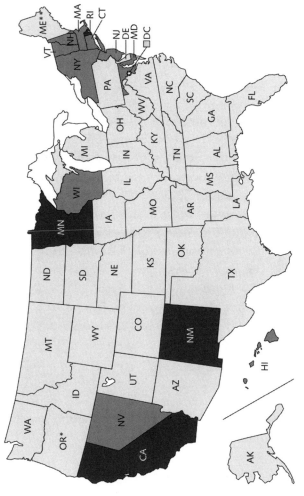

Laws banning discrimination based on sexual orientation and gender identity (4 states)

Minnesota (1993); Rhode Island (2001); New Mexico (2003); California (2003)

Laws banning discrimination based on sexual orientation (10 states):

Wisconsin (1982); Massachusetts (1989); Connecticut, and Hawaii (1992); New Jersey and Vermont (1992); New Hampshire (1997); Nevada (1999); Maryland (2001); New York (2002).

* An Oregon appellate court ruled that the state law prohibiting sex discrimination in the workplace also covers sexual orientation.

** Activists in Maine have twice passed a statewide nondiscrimination bill. The first—passed in 1997—was repealed by a 1998 ballot measure. The second—passed in 2000—automatically put the measure up for a public vote for ratification. On Nov. 7, 2000, Maine voters defeated the ballot initiative, invalidating the measure.

Support for equal treatment of gay people in most policy areas is now a mainstream American value.

Equal treatment of gay and lesbian people enjoys majority support in all areas except parenting and partner recognition, where the country is split down the middle—with about half supporting adoption, civil unions, and marriage, and half opposing these policies. The U.S. public supported "legally sanctioned partnerships and unions" for gay couples by a plurality of 47% to 42%, according to a 2001 poll.[40] A March 2002 ABC News poll found that a plurality of respondents support gay and lesbian adoption, 47% to 42%.[41] In a spring 2003 poll the public was evenly divided on civil unions, with 49% supportive and 49% opposed.[42] While nationally only two in five Americans support the freedom of same-sex couples to marry, and support for same-sex partner protections dropped in the wake of the pro-marriage Ontario court ruling and the pro-gay *Lawrence v. Texas* ruling in June 2003, overall the level of support for partner recognition and marriage has increased, and the level of opposition has decreased, over the past decade. The November 2004 National Election Poll found that one-quarter of voters support marriage equality for same-sex couples. Another one-third support civil unions. Only one in three voters opposes any legal protections for gay couples.[43]

While opposition to same-sex marriage is still persistent, strong majorities support equal access to the specific benefits of marriage. In short, support for equal treatment of gay people in most policy areas is now a mainstream American value—and local and state governments all over the country are leading the way in passing laws that embody this value.

The Emergence of a Gay Voting Bloc

Openly gay voters comprise a bloc equivalent in size to the Latino voting bloc.

During the past decade, the openly gay, lesbian, and bisexual vote emerged as a sizable, discrete voting bloc of 4% to 5% of the vote in national congressional and presidential elections.[44] This is equivalent in size to the Latino vote, and about half the size of the African American vote. While 14%

of gay voters backed George H. W. Bush in 1992, and fully 25% of gay voters supported George W. Bush in 2000, gay voters are the third most loyal Democratic voting bloc after African American and Jewish voters.[45] In 2004, 77% of gay voters backed Kerry, while 23% backed Bush. It is likely that close to 10% of Democratic primary voters are gay, lesbian, or bisexual.[46] In a close election, gay votes can make the difference between victory and defeat.

In a close election, gay votes can make the difference between victory and defeat.

ANTI-GAY POLITICS IN THE 1992 PRESIDENTIAL ELECTION

Even as America largely embraced gay equality during the 1990s—at least in terms of local and state policies and public opinion support for legal equality in most areas— at the same time anti-gay politics played an increasingly central role in presidential elections, particularly in 1992 and 1996. President Reagan came to power in part through the votes and money of religious conservatives, and both he and Vice President Bush relied upon their electoral support. Yet to a great extent, the Reagan–Bush approach to the religious right's opposition to gay rights and abortion was merely lip service—expressions of support and some significant policy changes (the gag rule regarding abortion counseling, continued anti-gay purges in the military), but little in the way of proactive "leadership." Religious right voters were a crucial part of the Reagan–Bush coalition, but they could also be taken for granted since they didn't have anywhere else to go.

This changed with the candidacy of Rev. Pat Robertson, whose 1988 presidential campaign had as its core "opposition to abortion and homosexuality," as the televangelist declared upon the announcement of his candidacy.[47] After a series of primary defeats, Robertson withdrew, but his list of campaign contributors served as the foundation for the Christian Coalition, which he launched in 1989. The coalition's membership soon grew to 3 million supporters

With contributors to his failed campaign, Robertson launched the Christian Coalition in 1989. He has since played a key role in the religious right influence on Republican politics.

and has played a key role in the religious right dominance of the Republican Convention of 1992, the Contract with America of 1994, and its influence on national Republican politics for more than a decade.

The central role of gay rights controversies during the 1992 presidential campaign, at least through the Republican Convention, is testament to the strength of the religious right within the Republican Party. This strength is disproportionately evident during primary elections and caucuses, when conservative and reactionary activists dominate.[48] President Bush's reelection campaign was foundering due to economic recession and other factors, and homophobia served as the glue that held together the otherwise fractious Republican Party. Richard Land, head of the Christian Life Commission of the Southern Baptist Convention, said at the time, "There is greater unanimity [on homosexuality] than even on the abortion issue."[49]

The state of Washington's 1992 Republican Party platform called for a ban on the employment of gays or lesbians as teachers or health-care workers. Iowa's Republican platform demanded the "rigid" enforcement of sodomy laws and mandatory reporting of the names of those who test positive for HIV. The national Republican Party platform called for contact tracing for HIV-positive people and stated the party's opposition to sexual orientation nondiscrimination legislation, adoption by gay parents, and gay marriage.[50]

Meanwhile, Arkansas Governor Bill Clinton was telling gays and lesbians on the campaign trail that he would reverse the ban on openly gay people in the military and launch a "Manhattan Project on AIDS." Governor Clinton, who had done nothing to move gay equality forward in Arkansas,[51] now ran to the left, telling teary-eyed gay audiences, "We don't have a person to waste" and "I have a vision and you are part of it."[52] Openly gay speakers at the Democratic Convention and a sea of "Lesbian Rights Now" signs from the National Organization for Women brought gay rights issues into America's living rooms.

Hostility toward gays set the tone of the Republican Convention in Dallas in August 1992. Gay rights and AIDS activists clashed with conservative activists and police outside the Houston Astrodome. Inside, Pat Buchanan denounced "the amoral idea that gay and lesbian couples should have the same standing in law as married men and women." He also ridiculed Clinton's support for gay equality to a receptive crowd, many of whom held signs reading "Family Values Forever, Gay Rights Never." Buchanan advocated a "culture war" against secular humanism and those advocating tolerance for various differences. Among at least six other speakers who echoed Buchanan's call were Education Secretary William Bennett, who devalued gay people and spoke against gay marriage. "Within very broad limits people may live as they wish," he said. "And yet we believe that some ways of living are better than others—better because they bring more meaning to our lives; to the lives of others; and to our fragile, fallible human condition. Marriage must be upheld because in marriage between husband and wife—and in fatherhood and motherhood —come blessings that cannot be won in any other way."[53] Vice President Dan Quayle directly mentioned gays in his acceptance speech: "Americans try to raise their children to understand right and wrong, only to be told that every so-called lifestyle is morally equivalent. That is wrong."[54] Finally, Republican National Committee Chairman Rich Bond explained to the press, "We are America; they are not America."[55] The Republicans' strategy failed, however, as the polls showed—a *New York Times* poll right after the convention found that only 23% of voters considered homosexuality an important election issue.[56] Clinton's mantra, "It's the economy, stupid," was a better indicator of the sentiment of voters still trying to escape the depths of recession. Despite the desire of many in the Republican Party to make Clinton's support for lifting the military ban a campaign issue, campaign aides resisted this, fearing further backlash like that evoked by the rhetorical excesses of the Houston convention.[57] In the end, Clinton won primarily due to economic discontent and a desire for new leadership. Lesbians and gays raised more than $3 million for Clinton–Gore, one-eighth of the total $25 million raised by the ticket. Three in four gays voted Democratic, and only 14% for President Bush.[58]

1996: "DEFENDING" MARRIAGE

Gay and lesbian couples have been challenging their exclusion from marriage laws since 1971.[59] However, it is only since the early 1990s that gay marriage has emerged as an issue of national political interest. In 1993, the Hawaii Supreme Court launched an important and ongoing international debate when it ruled that it was impermissible gender discrimination under the state constitution to deny three lesbian and gay couples the right to obtain a marriage license.[60] This decision stated that Hawaii could only deny the marriage licenses if it could indicate a compelling reason to do so. In 1996, a Hawaiian circuit court found that the state had failed to justify its denial with a compelling reason and so the couples must be allowed to marry under civil law. The court recognized that "Gay and lesbian parents and same-sex couples can be as fit and loving parents as non-gay men and women and different sex couples. . . . Same-sex couples can, and do, have successful, loving and committed relationships. . . . Gay men and lesbian women share this same mix of reasons for wanting to be able to marry" as heterosexual couples.[61] Judge Kevin Chang, who wrote the decision, concluded that the state "has failed to establish or prove that the public interest in the well-being of children and families, or the optimal development of children[,] will be adversely affected by same-sex marriage."[62]

Anti-gay activists and politicians made gay marriage a central issue in the 1996 presidential campaign. In January activists held a rally denouncing same-sex marriage just before the Iowa caucuses, the first primary election event. Nearly every Republican candidate attended and signed a pledge to "defend" heterosexual marriage against the threat allegedly posed by three lesbian and gay couples in Hawaii who had sued the state for the right to marry. The presidential candidates' anti-gay rhetoric quickly transformed mainstream state and national politics. By April 1996, the *Los Angeles Times* observed that "homosexual marriage has abruptly emerged as an emotional flashpoint in the debate about America's cultural mores."[63] Anti-gay groups became vocal once again, making claims such as Concerned Women for America's Beverly LaHaye's that "every local, state and federal law will be changed to accommodate homosexual 'marriage.'" During the 1996 debate, LaHaye claimed, falsely, that the legalization of same-sex marriage would force churches to marry gay couples. LaHaye also voiced fears that "homosexual 'marriage' would cause massive financial, legal and social upheaval as laws are revised to include same-sex partners. . . . Our entire system of government will be overhauled to include homosexuality as an approved and legal lifestyle."[64] Against this backdrop, presidential candidate Senator Bob Dole introduced the federal Defense of Marriage Act (DOMA), which was signed into law in August 1996. President Clinton not only signed the bill, he bragged about doing so in ads run on Christian radio stations. Dole also returned a $10,000 donation from the Log Cabin Republicans, a gay Republican organization.

During the 1996 presidential race, candidate Senator Bob Dole introduced the federal DOMA.

THE 2000 ELECTION CAMPAIGN

Throughout the 1999–2000 presidential primary, all ten of the Republican candidates opposed all of the major policy priorities of the gay, lesbian, bisexual, and trans-gender movement, except for a few who said they would appoint people to their administration regardless of sex-ual orientation. Echoing the 1996 anti-marriage rally, in August 1999, six of the Republican candidates signed on to an anti-gay pledge on the eve of the Iowa straw poll, pledging to oppose domestic partner benefits, education to fight anti-gay harassment and violence in the schools, adoption by gay people, and other issues.[65]

In the latter half of 1999, a slew of articles appeared in the mainstream press describing a more gay-friendly mainstream Republicanism.[66] Within the Republican Party, the most anti-gay, conservative candidates faded early on, while those who rose to the top tier—Senator John McCain and Governor George W. Bush—espoused a more subtle anti-gay politics. McCain in particular called for a more inclusive Republican Party, and said he was "proud" to meet with Log Cabin Republicans. Mc-Cain had, however, voted against the Employment Nondiscrimination Act in 1996.

In December 1999, the marriage issue arose again in the wake of the Vermont Supreme Court's ruling that the state must provide to same-sex couples every benefit and protection it provides to married heterosexual couples. Democratic candidates Bill Bradley and Al Gore, who sought the gay community's vote, applauded the deci-sion, while the Republican candidates denounced it. Re-ligious right activist Gary Bauer called the ruling "worse than terrorism."[67]

Throughout 2000, Governor Bush continued to artic-ulate anti-gay positions when asked. In South Carolina, he told a Christian radio station that he probably wouldn't appoint gays to his administration because "an openly known homosexual is somebody who probably wouldn't share my philosophy."[68] When first elected governor of Texas, Bush made a similar statement. There were no openly gay or lesbian members of his administration, and during his term, Bush defended Texas's sodomy law as "a symbolic gesture of traditional values,"[69] opposed sex education, and sought to tax condoms as a vice.[70] Throughout 1999 and 2000, Bush spoke out against gay adoption, same-sex marriage, hate crimes legislation, nondiscrimination laws, and sex education. Despite this, the Log Cabin Republicans reportedly spent $500,000 campaigning for Bush's election.

Vice Presidential nominee Dick Cheney—who had an extremely conservative voting record while a Congressman in the 1970s and 1980s, including votes against AIDS funding and the gathering of hate crimes statistics—pleasantly surprised many gay voters when he said same-sex partners should be able to enter into relationships and that states should be able to decide whether or not to recognize such relationships.[71] Such states' rights—usually a core tenet of conservative philosophy— were restricted by the federal DOMA, which Cheney and Bush support.

Despite Bush and Cheney's bottom-line adherence to anti-gay policy positions, the 2000 Republican Convention set a markedly different tone from its predecessors. A racially diverse array of speakers addressed an overwhelmingly white crowd of delegates. Perhaps the only note of discord came when gay Congressman Jim Kolbe spoke on international trade, and some delegates, in an anti-gay protest, bowed their heads to pray for Kolbe's soul. Also, despite the efforts of Wisconsin Governor Tommy Thompson, anti-gay language was kept in the Republican Party platform.

During his term as governor, Bush defended Texas's sodomy law as "a symbolic gesture of traditional values," opposed sex education, and sought to tax condoms as a vice.

The 2004 Republican and
Democratic Platforms on Lesbian and Gay Issues

While there are many key issues on which the two major parties disagree, their attitudes toward policy issues affecting lesbian and gay people represent one of the most striking areas of disagreement. Here are gay-related excerpts from the most recently available party platforms:

2004 REPUBLICAN PARTY PLATFORM
(http://www.gop.com/media/2004platform.pdf)

Same-Sex Marriage

"We strongly support President Bush's call for a Constitutional amendment that fully protects marriage, and we believe that neither federal nor state judges nor bureaucrats should force states to recognize other living arrangements as equivalent to marriage. We believe, and the social science confirms, that the well-being of children is best accomplished in the environment of the home, nurtured by their mother and father anchored by the bonds of marriage. We further believe that legal recognition and the accompanying benefits afforded couples should be preserved for that unique and special union of one man and one woman which has historically been called marriage.

"After more than two centuries of American jurisprudence, and millennia of human experience, a few judges and local authorities are presuming to change the most fundamental institution of civilization, the union of a man and a woman in marriage. Attempts to redefine marriage in a single state or city could have serious consequences throughout the country, and anything less than a Constitutional amendment, passed by the Congress and ratified by the states, is vulnerable to being overturned by activist judges. On a matter of such importance, the voice of the people must be heard. The Constitutional amendment process guarantees that the final decision will rest with the American people and their elected representatives. President Bush will also vigorously defend the Defense of Marriage Act, which was supported by both parties and passed by 85 votes in the Senate. This common sense law reaffirms the right of states not to recognize same-sex marriages licensed in other states.

"President Bush said, 'We will not stand for judges who undermine democracy by legislating from the bench and try to remake America by court order.' The Republican House of Representatives has responded to this challenge by passing H.R. 3313, a bill to withdraw jurisdiction from the federal courts over the Defense of Marriage Act. We urge Congress to use its Article III power to enact this into law, so that activist federal judges cannot force 49 other states to approve and recognize Massachusetts' attempt to redefine marriage."

Military Ban

"We affirm traditional military culture, and we affirm that homosexuality is incompatible with military service."

International Institutions

"Republicans continue to oppose the ideological campaign against participation by the Vatican in United Nations conferences and other activities. . . . Any effort to address global social problems must be firmly placed within a context of respect for the fundamental social institutions of marriage and family. We reject any treaty or convention that would contradict these values. For that reason, we support protecting the rights of families in international programs and oppose funding organizations involved in abortion."

"Activist, Hard-Left Judges"

"In the federal courts, scores of judges with activist backgrounds in the hard-left now have lifetime tenure. Recent events have made it clear that these judges threaten America's dearest institutions and our very way of life. In some states, activist judges are redefining the institution of marriage. . . . A Republican Congress, working with a Republican president, will . . . [use] Article III of the Constitution to limit federal court jurisdiction; for example, in . . . potential actions invalidating the Defense of Marriage Act (DOMA)."

2004 DEMOCRATIC PARTY PLATFORM
(http://www.democrats.org/pdfs/2004platform.pdf)

Same-Sex Marriages and States' Rights

"We support full inclusion of gay and lesbian families in the life of our nation and seek equal responsibilities, benefits, and protections for these families. In our country, marriage has been defined at the state level for 200 years, and we believe it should continue to be defined there. We repudiate President Bush's divisive effort to politicize the Constitution by pursuing a 'Federal Marriage Amendment.' Our goal is to bring Americans together, not drive them apart."

Employment Nondiscrimination

"We will enact the bipartisan legislation barring workplace discrimination based on sexual orientation."

Hate Crimes

"Racial and religious profiling is wrong and we will work to stamp it out. Hate crimes desecrate sacred spaces and demean good people, and we support a strong national law to punish them."

HIV/AIDS

"We will also work to ensure that people with HIV and AIDS have the care they need, and we will support the community-based prevention programs, built on experience with real life, that President Bush has cut."

Military Ban

"We are committed to equal treatment of all service members and believe all patriotic Americans should be allowed to serve our country without discrimination, persecution, or violence."

THE BUSH–CHENEY ADMINISTRATION

Under the banner of "compassionate conservatism," President George W. Bush has successfully positioned himself and his administration as moderate on a number of issues, including issues of concern to lesbians and gay men. President Bush often cultivates an image of tolerance by offering contradictory statements on particular issues. For example, on October 3, 2003, Bush signed an official proclamation designating the week of October 12 through October 18, 2003, as "Marriage Protection Week," declaring, "Marriage is a sacred institution, and its protection is essential to the continued strength of our society. . . . Marriage is a union between a man and a woman."[75] During the same week that President Bush endorsed the anti-gay Marriage Protection Week, he sent congratulations to the gay Metropolitan Community Church (MCC) on the occasion of the congregation's 35th anniversary. Nationwide, MCC churches perform more than 6,000 same-sex weddings annually.[76] However, Bush's largely anti-gay policy record is clear.

Bush's record on gay issues is not completely negative. Upon taking office in 2001, he did not repeal President Clinton's 1998 executive order banning sexual orientation discrimination in the federal civilian workforce. After a U.S. special counsel questioned whether the executive order mandated sexual orientation nondiscrimination in federal employment and after references to the law were removed from federal government websites, a Bush spokesperson promised that the administration would enforce the executive order against anti-gay discrimination.[77] Also, despite the concerns noted on the next page, the federal health bureaucracy has continued to fund some research and services that address health disparities correlated with sexual orientation.

George W. Bush's Anti-Gay Policy Record

- He opposes marriage equality for same-sex couples and supports amending the U.S. Constitution to define marriage only as a union of one man and one woman.

- Bush opposes the adoption of children by gay and lesbian families,[78] and his promotion of heterosexual marriage and fatherhood as solutions to child poverty sends the message that only heterosexual married couples are fully suited for raising children.[79]

- He opposes nondiscrimination laws[80] and hate crimes legislation[81] that include sexual orientation.

- Bush continues to support the military's "Don't Ask, Don't Tell" policy, which prohibits lesbian, gay, and bisexual people from openly serving in the U.S. armed forces.[82]

- He opposes age-appropriate, research-based sex education and has increased funding for abstinence-only-until-marriage sex education. These programs teach that sex outside the context of marriage is inherently dangerous, both physically and psychologically, and essentially tell gay and lesbian people that they should remain abstinent throughout their lives, since they cannot get married.[83]

- Bush has nominated numerous anti-gay judges and has appointed federal officials who are openly hostile to gay people.[84]

- He has advocated allowing faith-based service providers to ignore local and state nondiscrimination laws that include sexual orientation or gender identity when hiring for positions paid for with federal funds.[85]

- The Bush Administration has conducted costly and time-consuming audits of AIDS service organizations.[86] In 2003, National Institutes of Health (NIH) staff warned researchers to avoid certain terms connected with homosexuality in federal grant proposals to avoid extra scrutiny.[87] And, in October 2003, the Traditional Values Coalition, an anti-gay, right wing religious organization, prompted the U.S. Department of Health and Human Services to audit 250 research projects funded by NIH that involved issues related to sex or sexuality.[88]

Bush on Marriage Equality

For much of 2003 and into early 2004, Bush sent mixed messages about the Federal Marriage Amendment to the Constitution, which was first introduced in 2003 (see chapter 1 for a detailed history). Supporters of marriage equality for same-sex couples were somewhat buoyed when, on July 2, 2003, Bush said of the FMA, "I don't know if it's necessary yet . . . what I do support is a notion that marriage is between a man and a woman."[89] However, at a press conference in late July 2003, in which he was asked about the misleading and inaccurate statement in his State of the Union address that Iraq had tried to purchase uranium in Africa, Bush also announced his intention to introduce legislation that would further codify the ban on same-sex marriage.[90]

Bush has repeatedly denounced the November 2003 Massachusetts Supreme Judicial Court ruling legalizing marriage for same-sex couples,[91] for example, in his January 2004 State of the Union address.[92] After the Massachusetts Supreme Judicial Court ruled February 4, 2004, that civil unions would not provide equality to same-sex couples and reaffirmed the right of gay couples to marry under the Massachusetts Constitution's equality and due process guarantees, Bush called the ruling "deeply troubling" and reiterated his statement from the State of the Union address.[93] Later that month, he called gay marriages in San Francisco "troubling."[94] Finally, in late February 2004, he officially endorsed an anti-gay marriage amendment, calling on Congress to quickly pass such a measure.

Bush on More Limited Forms of Partner Recognition

In 2000, Bush said, "In the private sector [domestic partner benefits] are perfectly fine." On the governmental level, he said, the decision should be left up to cities and states.[95] However, as Governor of Texas, Bush took no initiative to offer domestic partner benefits to state employees or to create a domestic partner registry for Texas residents. Bush has not indicated whether or not he supports domestic partner benefits for same-sex partners of federal employees. Such a bill was introduced into Congress in 2003, but has gone nowhere.[96]

When White House Press Secretary Scott McClellan was asked how the president feels about the "concept of civil unions as an alternative to gay marriage," McClellan responded that Bush supports the Defense of Marriage Act, which "states that other states don't have to recognize the civil unions or same-sex marriages of other states. So his position is very clear in support of that."[97] Texas, which Bush used to lead as governor, does not offer civil unions to same-sex couples. And Bush endorsed Marriage Protection Week in October 2003, during which elected officials were asked to sign a pledge opposing not only marriage but also domestic partnership and civil unions for gay couples. In the 2000 debate with Senator Joseph Lieberman, Vice President Dick Cheney defended the right of gay couples to protect their relationships and defended states' rights to devise whatever form of partner recognition they might choose. In early 2004, Cheney reversed this position and endorsed President Bush's call for a constitutional amendment banning same-sex marriage. The proposed Federal Marriage Amendment would also prevent court rulings like the one in Vermont that prompted the state legislature to create civil unions.

The Bush Administration has not taken a clear stance on the provision of Social Security survivor and spousal benefits for same-sex couples. However, Bush and Cheney's apparent support for the Federal Marriage Amendment would preempt any court ruling in favor of equal treatment of same-sex couples under Social Security policy. On June 24, 2002, President Bush signed the Mychal Judge Act, named after the New York City Fire Department chaplain who was killed during the 9/11 terrorist attacks.[98] The bill allows same-sex partners of public safety officers killed in the line of duty to receive federally guaranteed life insurance benefits as long as the same-sex partners were designated as beneficiaries by their partners. The bill, however, is only retroactive to September 11, 2001.[99]

In August 2004, Vice President Cheney said that he differed with President Bush on the Federal Marriage Amendment. He said he personally opposed the measure but supported Bush's position out of loyalty to the president. One week before the November 2, 2004, election, President Bush said in an interview that he supported civil unions. This monumental "flip-flop" reversed Bush's earlier endorsement of Marriage Protection Week and the federal amendment, both of which call for a ban of civil unions, yet the media failed to note this glaring inconsistency, and Bush appeared more moderate and reasonable on gay issues.

THE WHITE HOUSE DEFENDS ITS POSITION

In support of their anti–same-sex marriage position, President Bush and fellow Republicans have raised particular defenses often repeated in the media. Along with promoting the FMA, they propose alternate paths that, they claim, will ensure gay people equal rights. These arguments are unfounded by fact and disproven by history.

Judicial Tyranny

In his 2004 State of the Union address, President Bush portrayed the Massachusetts Supreme Judicial Court as an antidemocratic rogue elephant run amok: "Activist judges . . . have begun redefining marriage by court order, without regard for the will of the people and their elected officials . . . the people's voice must be heard. If judges insist on forcing their arbitrary will upon the people, the only alternative left to the people would be the constitutional process."[100] When announcing his support for a constitutional amendment banning gay marriage a month later, Bush denounced "activist judges . . . [who] have made an aggressive attempt to redefine marriage."[101]

Bush's denunciation of activist judges is ironic given the role a bitterly divided U.S. Supreme Court played in his ascendancy to office. The 5-4 *Bush v. Gore* ruling of December 2000 ignored the will of the American people as expressed in the popular vote and, many would argue, possibly the will of Florida voters and thereby the Electoral College. But Bush's charge of judicial tyranny in the Bay State also echoes a broader theme that recurs frequently in this debate. The day after Massachusetts' high court legalized marriage for gay couples, U.S. House Majority Leader Tom Delay pushed the U.S. Constitutional ban, arguing that it is the only option "when you have a runaway judiciary that has no consideration of the Constitution of the United States."[102] Other conservative politicians and activists have echoed these claims. Family Research Council President Tony Perkins calls allegedly activist judges "the black plague."[103] Following the *Lawrence v. Texas* ruling striking down sodomy laws, one conservative columnist called for the impeachment of "the Sodomy 6."[104] In November 2003, the Catholic Action League called on the Massachusetts state legislature to impeach and convict for "abuse of office" the four justices who voted for marriage equality for same-sex couples, so the governor could appoint new justices "who will respect their oath of office."[105] In the wake of the *Lawrence* and *Goodridge* decisions, as well as the federal court–ordered removal of a monument of the Ten Commandments from Alabama's Supreme Court, the Traditional Values Coalition issued "A Call to End Judicial Tyranny!" This call urged Congress to cut the salaries of "renegade judges and their staffs," impeach them or abolish their positions, replace appointed state judiciaries with elected ones, and pass a law prohibiting the U.S. Supreme Court from ruling on homosexuality, abortion, and other right wing policy priorities.[106] Bills restricting courts from ruling in certain areas have already been introduced in some state legislatures. Such proposals would overturn the principle of judicial review established two centuries ago in *Marbury v. Madison*.

Some facts: Six of the seven Massachusetts Supreme Judicial Court judges, and three of the four so-called renegade judges in the majority, were appointed by Republican governors. Seven of the nine U.S. Supreme Court justices were appointed by Republican presidents. Of 13 federal appeals courts, nine have majorities of Republican appointees, two have majorities of Democratic appointees, and two are split evenly between Republican and Democratic appointees. Courts have also struck down environmental regulations, campaign finance

Six of the seven Massachusetts Supreme Judicial Court judges, and three of the four so-called renegade judges in the majority, were appointed by Republican governors.

restrictions, gun control, and even parts of the Violence Against Women Act, all policies that enjoy strong public support. Court rulings have often gone against public opinion.

Let the People Decide

Anti-gay groups appeal to populist sentiment when they say that the people should be able to decide whether or not to grant gay people rights through an up or down vote on a ballot question. However, it runs counter to America's founding principles to suggest that majorities should be able to mete out or withhold rights to members of a stigmatized minority through a secret ballot vote. Founding father James Madison warned that "measures are too often decided, not according to the rules of justice and the rights of the minor party, but by the superior force of an interested and overbearing majority."[107] In other words, majority rule, unchecked, can lapse into majority tyranny. Many developments we look back upon as historical advances—such as court rulings against segregation or bans on interracial marriage—would likely not have been passed by a majority of voters had they been put to a popular vote at the time. Prejudice or ignorance should never determine public policy; imagine the outcome if a simple majority vote could decide the rights of individuals with disabilities, immigrants, women, members of religious or racial minorities, or people who don't own property. Anti-gay ballot measures such as that proposed for Massachusetts—in which whether to grant or withhold individual rights would be decided by the majority in a secret ballot—violate this fundamental principle.

Courts play a crucial role in countering the potential tyranny of the majority by focusing on basic rights protected by state and federal constitutions, regardless of the political ramifications or the prejudices of the day. Courts defend justice when they courageously stick with constitutional principles—as Massachusetts's high court did in the marriage case—without regard to the politics or the popularity of their decision. This is the American system of government at its best.

Let the States Decide

Bush argued that any amendment passed by Congress "should fully protect marriage while leaving the state legislatures free to make their own choices in defining legal arrangements other than marriage."[108] Anti-gay groups backing the Federal Marriage Amendment say that this amendment would allow state legislatures to pass domestic partner policies, which provide some of the benefits of marriage to gay couples, and civil union policies, which can provide a separate form of equality at the level of state policy but none of the federal benefits of marriage.[109]

Yet the policy decisions made by the states are open to challenge in state legislatures. The groups that claim that the FMA will not preclude partnership policies at the state level have themselves fought domestic partnership and civil union laws in several states. In 1998–1999, the American Center for Law and Justice, founded by the Christian Coalition's Rev. Pat Robertson, filed a lawsuit on behalf of the Catholic Action League of Massachusetts—a member of the Coalition for Marriage—to strike down Boston's municipal domestic partnership policy.[110] In 2003, the Center for Marriage Law and the Alliance Defense Fund, two other Coalition for Marriage members, filed a similar lawsuit against domestic partnership benefits in Portland, Maine.[111] The American Center for Law and Justice, the legal arm of Pat Robertson's Liberty University, and other anti-gay groups have challenged domestic partner policies throughout the country. The proposed FMA could deter state and local governments from offering domestic partner health insurance to their employees or registries for resident gay couples, to avoid the costly legal battles that come with policy challenges.

The groups that claim that the FMA will not preclude partnership policies at the state level have themselves fought domestic partnership and civil union laws in several states.

Same-Sex Marriage Violates Tradition

President Bush criticized the actions of the Massachusetts court and local officials in San Francisco and New Mexico by appealing to tradition: "After more than two centuries of American jurisprudence and millennia of human experience, a few judges and local authorities are presuming to change the most fundamental institution of civilization."[112] Many other elected officials make similar claims. The Family Research Council's Tony Perkins claims that supporters of marriage equality for same-sex couples "throw out 6,000 years of human history that says marriage is between a man and a woman."[113]

Cases Involving Challenges to
Local Domestic Partnership Benefit Programs
(Status as of October 2002)

Status	City	Case (date of last decision*)
Domestic Partnership Program Overturned—Final	Atlanta, GA	*McKinney v. City of Atlanta* (March 14, 1995; S. Ct.)
	Minneapolis, MN	*Lilly v. City of Minneapolis* (March 29, 1995; S. Ct.)
	Boston, MA	*Connors v. City of Boston* (July 8, 1999; S. Ct.)
	Arlington County, VA	*White v. Arlington County* (April 21, 2000; S. Ct.)
Domestic Partnership Program Overturned—On Appeal	Philadelphia, PA	*Devlin v. City of Philadelphia* (August 29, 2002; App. Ct.)
Domestic Partnership Program Upheld—Final	Atlanta, GA	*Morgan v. City of Atlanta* (November 3, 1997; S. Ct.)
	Pima County, AZ	*LaWall v. Pima County* (July 14, 1998; Ct. of Ap.)
	Santa Barbara, CA	*Jacks v. City of Santa Barbara* (January 13, 1999; no appealed)
	Denver, CO	*Schaefer & Tader v. City of Denver* (April 12, 1999; S. Ct.)
	Chicago, IL	*Crawford v. City of Chicago* (October 6, 1999; S. Ct.)
	New York City, NY	*Slattery v. City of New York* (February 29, 2000; Ct. of Ap.)
	Chapel Hill and Carrboro, NC	*Godley v. Town of Chapel Hill and Town of Carrboro* (May 16, 2000; not appealed)
	Broward County, FL	*Lowe v. Broward County* (April 4, 2001; S. Ct.)
	Vancouver, WA	*Heinsma v. City of Vancouver* (August 23, 2001; S. Ct.)
	Montgomery County, MD	*Tyma v. Montgomery County* (June, 2002; S. Ct.)

*Date is of last available opinion or the denial of a review by a higher court, whichever is most recent.

Source: Gossett, Charles. (1999, September 4). Dillon goes to court: Legal challenges to local ordinances providing domestic partnership benefits. Paper presented to the annual meeting of the American Political Science Association, Atlanta, GA. Updated in personal communication with Charles Gossett, October 2002.

Many historians have critically examined this claim that marriage has always been exclusively heterosexual, including John Boswell and E. Graff. Boswell argues and provides significant evidence that at one time, the Roman Catholic and Eastern Orthodox Churches not only sanctioned same-sex unions, but actually sanctified them in ceremonies quite similar to marriage ceremonies of opposite-sex couples.[114] Graff notes that what marriage means socially has changed dramatically over time. Marriage laws in the U.S. and Europe used to consider wives the property of their husbands. And over the course of history, other innovations—marriage for love instead of arranged marriages, marriages in which women work instead of stay at home, childless marriages, and interracial and interreligious marriages—have been portrayed as extreme threats to the institution that would lead to its destruction.[115]

American wives only earned the right to own property in 1887, after almost 50 years of legislative efforts in the states.[116] Well into the twentieth century, men could beat their wives with legal sanction. In 1911, the U.S. Supreme Court rejected an attempt by an abused wife to sue her husband, considering such a proposition "revolutionary" and "radical and far reaching." Abolitionist and suffragist Lucy Stone was right to state that "marriage is to woman a state of slavery."[117]

Those who cite the Bible in defense of "marriage between one man and one woman" are also exercising selective vision. Ron Grossman notes that many Jewish patriarchs and kings of the Old Testament were polygamous, like Solomon, who was reputed to have 700 wives. The practice of polygamy lasted "well into the Middle Ages" among Sephardic Jews in Arab countries.[118]

While some cultures persecuted homosexuality, others were more accepting. In the Greek city-state of Thebes, according to Plutarch, the elite force of the

At one time, the Roman Catholic and Eastern Orthodox Churches not only sanctioned same-sex unions, but actually sanctified them in ceremonies quite similar to marriage ceremonies of opposite-sex couples.

Thebean army consisted of 150 gay male couples. This battalion fought to the death of the last man against the Macedonians.[119] Aristotle and Siculus noted that the Celts—then inhabiting territrory north and west of Athens—widely tolerated and encouraged unions between two men.[120] There were no anti-gay laws in Ireland until they were introduced by England's Henry VIII in 1533, prescribing forfeiture of property and even death for "sodomites."[121] This is not to say that precolonial Ireland was a gay-tolerant paradise; but homosexuality was not a crime under the native Brehon legal code, as it became under the new English order.

"More than a century of anthropological research provides no support whatsoever for the view that either civilization or viable social orders depend upon marriage as an exclusively heterosexual institution."

The American Anthropological Association (AAA) called President Bush's conception of the history of marriage "patently false." The 11,000-member AAA's executive board said, "The results of more than a century of anthropological research on households, kinship relationships and families, across cultures and through time, provide no support whatsoever for the view that either civilization or viable social orders depend upon marriage as an exclusively heterosexual institution." Echoing Boswell, the anthropologists pointed to "sanctified same-sex unions in the fourth century in Christianity" and the practice of male-born berdaches marrying men in some Native American cultures.[122]

There are other traditions we can cite to support recognizing same-sex marriages, such as comity between states and nations. Comity is the tradition—obviously sometimes contested, as in the Tennessee interracial marriage noted in the first chapter—whereby marriages valid where celebrated are valid everywhere, even if they would not be celebrated in the other jurisdiction. In addition, the American tradition of jurisprudence is one of evolving understandings of citizenship and rights. When the founding fathers wrote "that all men are created equal, that they are endowed by their Creator with certain inalienable Rights, and that among these are Life, Liberty and the pursuit of Happiness," "all men" was not understood to include gay people. But at the same time, it was also understood to include only white male property owners. Our understanding of this principle has changed over time to include women, people of color, and non–property owners. These expansions of rights were justified through a broader understanding of the equal protection and due process provisions of the U.S. Constitution.

THE 2004 DEMOCRATIC PRESIDENTIAL CANDIDATES: THE MOST PRO-GAY FIELD YET

The ten Democratic presidential candidates who ran in 2003 and 2004 were by far the most pro-gay field of candidates ever. All of the Democrats supported most of the key issues of concern to gay, lesbian, bisexual, and transgender people: sexual orientation nondiscrimination laws, HIV/AIDS prevention and treatment, lifting the military ban, hate crimes laws, domestic partnership, and gay-supportive education policy.[123] The few differences among the candidates were regarding marriage and civil unions.

Three of the nine candidates still in the race in January 2004—former U.S. Senator and Ambassador Carol Moseley Braun, Congressman Dennis Kucinich, and the Rev. Al Sharpton—supported full marriage equality for same-sex couples. The other six candidates did not unequivocally support marriage equality. Four of these six—Senator John Edwards, Representative Dick Gephardt, Senator John Kerry, and Senator Joseph Lieberman—repeatedly expressed their opposition to marriage for same-sex couples. At the same time, these four spoke out against the Federal Marriage Amendment and made supportive comments in the wake of the Massachusetts court ruling.

The other two candidates, retired General Wesley Clark and former Vermont Governor Howard Dean, did not say they opposed marriage for gay couples. However, on numerous occasions, when asked if they support marriage, they answered that they support civil unions. They also expressed support for the recent Massachusetts ruling in favor of marriage equality, saying it reflected concern for "rights" (Clark) and "equality" (Dean) for all Americans regardless of sexual orientation.[124]

Senator John Kerry, the 2004 Democratic candidate, opposes marriage and supports civil unions. He frequently stated his opposition to the Federal Marriage Amendment, but also expressed support for an anti-gay marriage constitutional amendment pending to the Massachusetts state constitution. The amendment first introduced in the Massachusetts legislature was a Super-DOMA that would not only ban marriage, but threaten more limited forms of recognition such as domestic partnership. In March 2004, this amendment was rejected by the legislature in favor of a different amendment that would ban marriage but legalize civil unions. Kerry announced his support for the Massachusetts constitutional amendment while campaigning in Ohio, which had just passed a Super-DOMA law weeks earlier. Kerry's position is therefore inconsistent, in that he opposes such a measure in the U.S. Congress, where he sits, but supports such a measure in the Massachusetts legislature. Kerry later expressed support for the anti-marriage amendment passed overwhelmingly by voters in Missouri in August 2004.

GAY MARRIAGE AND THE 2004 PRESIDENTIAL ELECTION

In the wake of President Bush's close reelection over Senator Kerry in November 2004, a new conventional wisdom emerged. This widespread assumption held that John Kerry lost the 2004 presidential election because of gay marriage, particularly because of an anti-marriage amendment on the Ohio ballot. *Newsweek* reported that Bill Clinton warned Kerry to come out strongly against the anti-family amendments on the ballot in 11 states on November 2. On the Sunday morning talk shows on November 14, Clinton called the anti-marriage amendments "an overwhelming factor" in Kerry's loss.

It is a gross overstatement to say that Kerry lost because of gay marriage. While gay marriage was an issue in the 2004 elections, it was only one of many concerns motivating voters. The following facts complicate what seems to be a simple calculus:

- Eight of the 11 states with anti-gay marriage amendments on the ballot have gone Republican in most or all of the recent presidential elections.
- Three battleground states had anti-family amendments. Kerry won two of these—Michigan and Oregon—even as voters there approved anti-gay marriage amendments. Kerry won Oregon 51% to 47%, while Al Gore barely carried it 47% to 47%. Kerry matched Gore's share of the Michigan vote—51%—but won 288,513 more votes than Gore did there in 2000.
- The third battleground state with an anti-marriage amendment, Ohio, went Republican in four of the last six elections. Since 1980, only Bill Clinton has been able

to win Ohio for the Democrats. Going into the 2004 election, Ohio was "leaning Republican."

- Kerry won 473,474 more votes in Ohio than Al Gore won in 2000 there. Bush won 444,938 more votes in Ohio in 2004 than he won in 2000 there, when he carried the state. In other words, Kerry picked up 28,536 more votes over Gore's showing than Bush increased *his* showing by. Kerry's Ohio vote was 22% higher than what Gore got in 2000; Bush increased his 2004 vote by only 19% over his 2000 vote count there. But because Bush won the state in 2000 and was starting from a higher base of Republican votes, this 28,536 vote deficit didn't matter and Bush won the state.

- Like President Bush, Kerry and his running mate, Senator John Edwards, frequently voiced their opposition to gay marriage. Kerry endorsed anti-marriage amendments in his home state of Massachusetts and in Missouri.

Much has been made of the 22% of voters in the November 2, 2004, exit poll who said "moral values" drove their choice for president. But as Hunter College political scientist Ken Sherrill points out, most "moral values" voters are hard-core Republicans who overwhelmingly support the war in Iraq and think it is going well, and backed Republican Congressional candidates. Courting these voters is not a winning strategy for liberals and progressives.

The U.S. Constitution guarantees "equal protection of the laws" for all Americans —not just for heterosexual Americans, and not just for those who can win a popularity contest. Putting basic rights up for a majority vote is neither moral nor in the best traditions of this country. Denying loving and committed couples equal legal protections for their relationships and their children is not moral.

In a national poll of 1,000 voters conducted November 1–2, 2004, by Lake, Snell, Perry & Associates, only 2% said that "gay and lesbian rights issues" was the most important issue to them in deciding for whom to vote. The top issue was "jobs and the economy" (23%), followed by "homeland security and terrorism" (19%) and "Iraq" (13%). Only 10% cited "moral values" as their chief concern.

To say that the anti-family amendments on the ballots in 11 states cost Senator Kerry the election is simplistic and not warranted by the exit poll data. The anti-gay/anti-family amendments—which will deny health coverage to thousands of American families, gay and straight, many with children—were a factor in the outcome in Ohio, but not in Oregon, Michigan, or the other eight states. Even in Ohio, the anti-marriage amendment was only one of many factors in a close election.

Although anti-gay ballot measures are increasingly being rejected by voters, the anti-gay family movement has proposed several dozen anti-marriage ballot measures to be voted on between 2005 and 2006.

MAJORITY TYRANNY:
ANTI-FAMILY CONSTITUTIONAL AMENDMENTS

Following three decades of anti-gay activism by a well-funded anti-gay movement, marriage and family recognition issues affecting same-sex couples have played a recurrent and central role in U.S. presidential politics. Although there have been significant advances in legal equality for gay people, the anti-gay backlash has been effective. Forty states now ban same-sex marriage, and 15 of these ban other forms of partner recognition as well. (See map on p. 8.) Six states restrict the ability of gay men, lesbians, or same-sex couples to serve as foster and adoptive parents.[125] Most states have parental notification laws, which require written consent of parents before students can participate in classes in which topics such as sex, sexuality, and AIDS can be discussed.[126]

Although anti-gay ballot measures are increasingly being rejected by voters, the anti-gay family movement has proposed several dozen anti-marriage ballot measures around the country to be voted on between 2005 and 2006. Most of these would ban marriage for same-sex couples, and many would also ban more limited forms of partner recognition. For example, Wisconsin's amendment, which must be approved in a ballot referendum, would read:

> Only marriage between one man and one woman shall be valid or recognized as a marriage in this state. A legal status identical or substantially similar to that of marriage for unmarried individuals shall not be valid or recognized in this state.[127]

Little has changed since the first anti-gay ballot campaigns of the 1970s. Claims that gays can choose heterosexuality and that gay rights laws are "special rights" still inform policy formulation in the White House, the nation's highest courts, Congress, and state houses around the country. While culturally the U.S. is increasingly pro-gay, and while American voters, even Republicans, are largely supportive of most forms of legal equality for gays, politically speaking, the country remains profoundly anti-gay. The anti-gay movement has enormously influenced the Republican Party's position on gay rights issues, as well as Bush Administration policies regarding sex education, family policy, and even human rights advocacy in international arenas, where the administration has sided with theocratic Muslim nations and the Vatican against provisions recognizing the rights of women, children, and gay people. The Republican and Democratic Party platforms on gay issues keep the parties highly polarized. Due in part to the emergence of a strong movement for gay equality and a strong reaction to the social shifts this movement has achieved, gay rights issues—and especially gay marriage—remain a defining fault line in American politics.

The Case for Marriage Equality

Marriage aims to promote healthy families by protecting the economic and emotional interdependence of family members and giving priority to their bonds. Gay couples have the same needs as opposite-sex couples: same-sex couples are often emotionally and economically interdependent, sharing household and financial responsibilities, and they often raise children or take care of other family members together. Legal protection of partner relationships, which includes a comprehensive package of economic and social rights and responsibilities for couples and their children, provides families with security and peace of mind. A 2004 report by the U.S. General Accounting Office lists 1,138 ways in which marital relationships are given special treatment by the federal government.[1]

TWO STORIES

Described in chapter 2 (see p. 39) is the birth of the daughter of Julie and Hillary Goodridge, the lead plaintiffs in the Massachusetts lawsuit. What should have been a joyful occasion, with both mothers together welcoming their newborn child, turned into a "nightmare," as Julie underwent a caesarean section and little Annie was taken to the neonatal intensive care unit. Hillary, with legal ties to neither her partner nor her daughter, was prohibited by hospital staff from seeing either one.

The effects of being unable to marry are felt in families headed by same-sex couples throughout the country, in large and small ways. Being unable to marry has particularly devastating consequences when one partner dies. For the surviving partner, securing the basic right to the financial support the deceased partner contributed to their household—a right afforded to heterosexual couples through marriage—involves protracted battles with federal and state bureaucracies, at a time of great emotional strain, and often with little result.

Lois Marrero and Mickie Mashburn

In July 2001, Lois Marrero, an officer in the Tampa, Florida, Police Department, was killed while trying to stop a bank robbery. Mickie Mashburn, Lois's partner of 11 years and a 17-year veteran of the Tampa Police Department, grieved with Lois's family, with whom she had been close for 18 years. The night Lois was killed, Lois's sister told interviewers, "We love Mickie; she is part of our family." Lois and Mickie lived publicly as a lesbian couple. They had been joined in a public commitment ceremony ten years earlier and lived together and took care of one another. They educated the Tampa police force about gay and lesbian

issues. It was Lois's death, however, that made it clear that their relationship was not recognized in significant ways.

Although they had shared bills for years, Mickie was told she was not eligible for Lois's pension. She sued, but at the end of a bitter trial Lois's blood relatives took Lois's pension and left Mickie with nothing. "The money can't bring Lois back," Mickie says, "but we need to have this right for our relationships. No one else should go through what I have gone through. We need to be accepted like everyone else."[2] Had Mickie and Lois had the right to marry, they would have been able to protect their family and their right to inherit each other's pension in the event of an untimely death.

Larry Courtney and Eugene Clark

Larry Courtney and Eugene Clark moved together to New York from Washington, D.C., in 1988 so that Larry could accept a job offer. Larry and Eugene enjoyed life in New York. They reveled in the general acceptance of their gay relationship as a family unit. They entertained friends and family. They went to the theater. They went to some of the city's many gay bars. They vacationed together and spent holidays together with different family members or with friends. When Eugene's mother had a stroke in 1995, Eugene and Larry brought her from Washington to live with them in their small Manhattan apartment; they both nursed her and cared for her until she passed away in 1999. Eugene and Larry lived life as a married couple. In 1994, when it became legal, they registered in New York City as domestic partners, receiving a certificate that was as close to a marriage license as they would ever have.

On October 30, 2001, Eugene Clark and Larry Courtney would have celebrated 14 years as committed lifetime partners. On the morning of September 11, 2001, they got up early, had coffee together, and dressed for work. Eugene kissed Larry goodbye and said, "I'll see you tonight." He left a little earlier than usual so that he could vote in New York City's primary election before the polls got crowded. He then boarded the subway for the ride to his office at Aon Consulting on the 102nd floor of the South Tower of the World Trade Center.

At approximately 8:55 AM Larry arrived at his own office in midtown Manhattan to a voicemail message from Eugene that said, "Don't worry, the plane hit the other building. I'm OK. We are evacuating." At 9:03 AM a second hijacked plane hit the 86th floor of the South Tower. The building collapsed at 10:05 AM. Eugene did not come home.

After frantic searching of the streets and emergency rooms, and after posting his photograph along with the many others, Larry reported Eugene as a missing person at the Armory. He later filed an affidavit for a death certificate at the makeshift Family Center at Pier 94. Among a host of other paperwork Larry received in the mail were documents from Cambridge Integrated Services Group, Inc., for filing a workers' compensation claim. He sent the paperwork off and was summoned for a hearing in April 2002. At the hearing, Cambridge stated that Larry did not qualify for the benefits that Eugene's company had been paying for during his tenure because the couple did not fit the "legally married" criteria. The benefits could be paid to Eugene's surviving parent, his father. But Eugene had not seen or spoken to his father in over 20 years, and he had never spoken to Larry about him.

Larry decided to fight for his spousal rights and teamed up with the Lambda Legal Defense and Education Fund, which was advocating for many other surviving partners. They were ultimately successful, and New York State Senate Bill S7685 became law on August 20, 2002. The bill designated domestic partners as spouses of victims of 9/11, due full spousal benefits from workers' compensation. The bill is restricted to the 9/11 attacks, however. It does not protect same-sex spouses who lose partners in other tragedies.[3]

SURVIVING SAME-SEX PARTNERS AND THE AFTERMATH OF 9/11

Of the nearly 3,000 Americans and foreign nationals killed in the 9/11 terrorist attacks in New York, Washington, D.C., and Pennsylvania, many were gay, lesbian, or bisexual individuals in long-term, committed relationships like Larry and Eugene's. Because these were high-profile atrocities of international significance, the tragic losses these gay couples suffered were prominent. In the weeks and months following 9/11, moderate Republicans such as New York Mayor Rudy Giuliani and Governor George Pataki backed equal treatment of same-sex surviving partners. So too did the American Red Cross, the United Way of New York, and the U.S. Congress, which passed the Mychal Judge Police and Fire Chaplains Public Safety Officers' Benefit Act, named for Father Mychal Judge, the New York Fire Department chaplain killed while administering last rites to firefighters killed at the World Trade Center. Signed into law by President Bush on June 24, 2002, the law grants a one-time federal benefit of $250,000 to any designated beneficiary recognized under the deceased's police officer's or firefighter's life insurance plan. Prior to the Judge Act, the federal benefit was given only to spouses, children, and parents of officers who died in the line of duty. The Judge Act was retroactive only to September 11, 2001 (and so partners of police officers and firefighters killed in the line of duty prior to this date, such as Mickie Mashburn, cannot benefit).

Peggy Neff, whose partner of 18 years, Sheila Hein, was killed at the Pentagon on September 11, 2001, received compensation from the September 11 Victims Compensation Fund in January 2003. She was the first same-sex survivor to ever receive such compensation from the federal government.[4] Neff's case was strong in that Hein's will named her as the beneficiary. As of June 2004, the fund had just completed its distribution of funds. It was unclear exactly how approximately 20 other same-sex surviving partners of people killed in 9/11 had been treated by the fund. According to Eric Ferrero of Lambda Legal, other gay partners were given funds. Sometimes they split the money with parents, siblings, and other members of the victim's family of origin.

In 2004, approximately 20 same-sex surviving partners of people killed in 9/11 are still awaiting a decision from the federal fund.

The compassion shown to same-sex surviving partners after 9/11 was decried and challenged by organizations with an anti-gay agenda:

Robert Knight, director of Concerned Women for America's Culture and Family Institute, accused surviving partners like Larry Courtney and the gay advocates who helped him of "trying to hijack the moral capital of marriage and apply it to their own relationships," which he characterized as "counterfeit marriage." Cybercast News Service—a right wing website that frequently quotes religious right, anti-gay activists—reported that Knight said that "family benefits were originally created to provide for a stay-at-home parent caring for a child, not for homosexual sex partners who usually both work."[5]

After the American Red Cross decided to provide services to gay surviving partners of 9/11 victims, CWA criticized the group's "broad and inclusive definition of family."[6] CWA's Culture and Family Institute also censured the 45 members of Congress who urged Attorney General John Ashcroft to adopt a federal policy similar to that promoted by Governor Pataki in New York state, claiming that lawmakers and "homosexual activists" were exploiting the tragedy "to ask Ashcroft to pave way for 'domestic partner' benefits."[7]

Focus on the Family's James Dobson said, "Pataki diluted the definition of 'family' by giving gay partners the same access to terrorist relief benefits that married couples have."[8] FOF also criticized Pataki's actions as advancing the "gay agenda."[9]

The Traditional Values Coalition's Lou Sheldon accused gay activists of "taking advantage" of the national tragedy to promote their agenda. Sheldon urged that relief assistance be "given on the basis and priority of one man and one woman in a marital relationship."[10] Such a policy would have also left out unmarried opposite-sex partners of 9/11 victims. "We don't devalue the loss of these innocent people," Sheldon insisted, "but we think this is not the time to institutionalize such 'partnerships' and put them on the same level as marriage."[11]

Peter Sprigg of the Family Research Council also accused gays of "taking advantage of the grief and compassion that Americans do feel. . . . To redefine the family based on our grief over the losses that people may have experienced as a result of the terror attacks would be bad law and bad policy."[12]

Perhaps as a result of these objections, the initial interim regulations issued by the Department of Justice in December 2001 and the final regulations issued in March 2002 did not explicitly recognize same-sex partners, but instead left the states to determine who is eligible for victim's compensation under the federal fund.[13] However, most states do not provide any legal recognition to same-sex partners, even those in committed, long-term or lifelong relationships. As of March 2002, when the September 11th Fund issued its final regulations, none of the three states where the attacks occurred—New York, Pennsylvania, and Virginia— afforded any recognition to same-sex partners of state residents.[14]

As of March 2002, when the September 11th Fund issued its final regulations, none of the three states where the attacks occurred—New York, Pennsylvania, and Virginia— afforded any recognition to same-sex partners of state residents.

FOCUS ON THE FUTURE

Marriage rights for gay couples are no longer an abstract hypothetical. Hundreds, and perhaps thousands, of American gay and lesbian couples have married in Canada, and they are *married*. Thousands more have married in San Francisco, Oregon, New York, New Jersey, and now Massachusetts. These married gay couples will go about their lives and do the things other married couples do—apply for mortgages, seek health benefits for their spouses and children, and build a life together. Married Canadian couples will travel to the U.S. on vacation, to work, or to study. The American people have a choice in how they are going to treat these hopeful newlyweds. They can treat them with respect, dignity, and fairness, or they can discriminate against them. Hopefully, Americans will do the right thing.

Thousands of American gay and lesbian couples have married in Canada, California, Oregon, New York, New Jersey, and Massachusetts. The American people have a choice in how they are going to treat these hopeful newlyweds.

During the initial rush of same-sex marriages in San Francisco in early 2004, Mayor Gavin Newsom asked a compelling question. The 34-year-old Newsom had been married to his wife for two years. He pointed to the first couple married—Del Martin, 83, and Phyllis Lyon, 79, who have been together for half a century. "Why," he asked, "should we have more rights than them?" This is a critical question, and nicely sums up the issue facing legislators, opinion leaders, and the American public. Why should Del and Phyllis not be able to protect their home under the Medicaid spend-down provision if one of them has to go into a nursing home? Why should one be denied visiting the other in the hospital because a hospital staff member doesn't consider them family? When one of them dies, why shouldn't the other be able to access the extra income from her partner's Social Security survivor benefits? They paid into the system all their lives, the same as heterosexual Americans did.

Internationally, there is a distinct trend toward protecting the committed relationships of same-sex couples. For example, 14 countries, including South Africa, Israel, and Britain, protect same-sex couples

Internationally, there is a distinct trend toward protecting the committed relationships of same-sex couples. Two countries, the Netherlands and Belgium, have ended marriage discrimination against same-sex couples.[15] Canada is on the verge of doing this as well, with three provinces containing three-quarters of the country's population—Ontario, British Columbia, and Quebec—already marrying same-sex couples. Taiwan is considering legalizing same-sex marriage. Many other countries protect same-sex relationships. Brazil allows same-sex partners to inherit each other's pension and Social Security benefits. Tasmania, one of Australia's most conservative states, has created a broad domestic partnership status.[16] Worldwide, 14 countries, including South Africa, Israel, and Britain, protect same-sex couples for the purposes of immigration. Save for the Massachusetts Supreme Judicial Court ruling, the United States lags behind many allies in Europe and in several developing-world nations.

But public opinion may soon sway the debate. A slight majority of Massachusetts voters supports marriage equality.[17] Majorities in New Jersey, Connecticut, and New Hampshire also support marriage rights for same-sex couples.[18] Nearly five years ago, two-thirds (66%) of Americans said that same-sex marriage would be legalized in their lifetime.[19] A majority of Americans support equal access to the specific benefits of marriage: most people feel that gays and lesbians should be entitled to inheritance rights (73%) and Social Security survivor benefits (68%); 58% of U.S. college freshmen surveyed in 2001–2002 support same-sex marriage.[20]

While no national poll yet shows majority support for the legalization of same-sex marriage, and in fact significant majorities oppose it, the public is split on whether or not the U.S. Constitution should be amended to ban gay marriage.[21] And amending the Constitution is decidedly not a priority of the voting public: A February 2004 Pew Research Center poll found that only 22% of Americans considered passing a marriage amendment a top priority. In fact, the issue was ranked 21st in importance out of a total of 22 issues on the survey.[22]

A constitutional amendment banning gay marriage ranks 21st out of 22 issues of importance to Americans.

The United States of America stands at a critical historical juncture. A group of people who have been denied legal equality—in this instance, the right to state recognition and protection of their family relationships—are on the verge of achieving that legal equality, at least in Massachusetts. Depending on the outcome of forthcoming legal challenges, thousands of gay couples may have already achieved that equal protection in San Francisco and elsewhere. Gay couples have recently been granted legal equality in Ontario, British Columbia, and Quebec, which hold three-quarters of Canada's population. Thousands of gay and lesbian families, many of them raising children, will be able to sleep more soundly knowing that if they experience a health emergency or other family crisis, they can rely upon the structure of laws and policies that protect the married, heterosexual couple families most of us grew up in. People will be guaranteed their family integrity in the event of a catastrophe. When gay couples can marry in this country, America will have more closely approximated many of its most important animating principles: *e pluribus unum* (out of many, one); liberty and justice for all; the land of the free; equality and due process; fairness; compassion; tolerance. Gay couples will be safer. Gay families and their children will benefit. The changes in family policy under way in Massachusetts will hurt no one. If America embraces principles of fairness and compassion and grants gay and lesbian families equal protection under the law, future generations will look back on this moment in our history much like we reflect on other critical historical turning points—as a point in time when Americans had a choice and chose hope over fear, compassion over scapegoating, equality over exclusion, and fairness over injustice.

Afterword

For the past 15 years, I have worked to promote equality for gay, lesbian, bisexual, and transgender people and people with HIV/AIDS. For most of the 1990s, I did this in a volunteer capacity with a number of community-based organizations in Michigan, where I attended graduate school, and in my native Massachusetts. (Over the past 20 years I have also advocated in a volunteer capacity on a number of other issues, including environmental racism and classism, nuclear weapons, U.S. policy in Central America, and in support of peace and justice in Northern Ireland.) As I was researching and writing a political science dissertation on anti-gay politics in the U.S., I taught political science part-time, worked as an editor and journalist, and ran an anti-poverty and human services research and advocacy group.

For the last five years, I have had the privilege of working at the Policy Institute of the National Gay and Lesbian Task Force. The Policy Institute conducts social science research, policy analysis, and strategy development on issues of concern to gay, lesbian, bisexual, and transgender people. We work with a number of partners who are policymakers, researchers, service providers, and grassroots activists. We conduct research on a broad range of issues affecting gay people, including discrimination, parenting, elder and youth issues, health policy, and family recognition policy.

I wrote this book because I feel the current debate over marriage equality for same-sex couples is a critical policy debate that will have long-term implications. When gay and lesbian couples can marry in the U.S., their families and especially their children will be greatly helped, and no one will be hurt. In Massachusetts, at least 8,000 children being raised in same-sex couple households will be protected in the event of a family emergency. Gay and lesbian partners, and especially those who are parents, will sleep better at night knowing that if one of them becomes sick, is injured, or dies, their surviving partner and children will not have to fight the agonizing battles Larry Courtney and Mickie Mashburn had to fight (see their stories in chapter 5). They will be less likely to suffer the pain of being rejected by their partner's relatives, as Mickie Mashburn had to experience. They will know that even though anti-gay bias is still prevalent in society, their government—of the people, by the people, and for the people—will treat them with respect and compassion. Contrary to the false and alarmist claims of opponents of gay marriage, America will be a stronger and better place when gay and lesbian couples are allowed to protect their family relationships.

Notes

PREFACE

1. Preliminary data from Clarence Patton, deputy director, New York City's Gay and Lesbian Anti-Violence Project, in personal conversation, March 2, 2004.

2. This would not be the first time anti-gay activism coincided with a spike in anti-gay violence. In 1992, a lesbian and a gay man were killed after their Oregon home was firebombed just before voters considered an anti-gay ballot measure. The measure would have banned sexual orientation nondiscrimination legislation, prohibited state and local government agencies from providing services to organizations with such nondiscrimination policies, and declared homosexuality "abnormal, wrong, unnatural and perverse." The two people killed were active in the campaign to defeat the initiative.

CHAPTER 1

1. McClelland, C. (2003, June 18). Same-sex marriage endorsed in Canada; Government will act to change law. *Washington Post.* p. A22.

2. Krauss, C. (2003, June 15). Gay Canadians' quest for marriage seems near victory. *New York Times.*

3. Ibid.

4. McClelland, C. (2003, June 18).

5. *Sydney Morning Herald* (2003, July 10). Second Canadian province legalizes gay marriage.

6. Wockner, R. (2004, March 25). Quebec legalizes same-sex marriage. *The Weekly News* (Miami). www.theweeklynews.org/Archive_TWN/040325/040325_international_news.htm. Accessed June 13, 2004.

7. Dvorak, P. (2003, June 27). Gay community hails a "new day"; Ruling on sodomy law celebrated. *Washington Post*. p. B01.

8. Savage, D. (2003, June 28). Ruling seen as precursor to same-sex marriages; Supporters and foes of gay civil rights say the court's overturning of sodomy laws could lead to gay unions. *Los Angeles Times*. www.latimes.com. Accessed June 29, 2003.

9. Ibid.

10. Ibid.

11. Gearan, A. (2003, June 26). Scalia blasts court on sodomy ruling. Associated Press, www.ap.org. Accessed June 27, 2003.

12. Lewis, N. (2003, June 27). Conservatives furious over court's direction. *New York Times*. www.nytimes.com. Accessed June 28, 2003.

13. Santorum, R. (2003, July 9). Americans must preserve the institution of marriage. *USA Today*.

14. Savage (2003, June 28).

15. Harlow cited in Santorum (2003, July 9).

16. Belluck, P. (2003, November 19). Marriage by gays gains big victory in Massachusetts; Legislature told to clear way—Court cites state constitution. *New York Times*. pp. A1, A24.

17. *Goodridge v. Department of Public Health*, 440 Mass. 309, 342 (2003).

18. Lewis, R. (2004, February 5). SJC affirms gay marriage. *Boston Globe*. www.boston.com Accessed June 13, 2004.

19. *Baehr v. Lewin*, 852 P.2d 44 (Haw. 1993) (plurality).

20. "No State . . . shall be required to give effect to any public act, record, or judicial proceeding of any other State . . . respecting a relationship between persons of the same sex that is treated as a marriage under the laws of such other State . . . or a right or claim arising from such a relationship." Defense of Marriage Act of 1996, Pub. L. No. 104–199, 110 Stat. 2419 (1996). Cited in Lewis, G., and Edelson, J. (2000). DOMA and ENDA: Congress votes

on gay rights. In Rimmerman, C., Wald, K., and Wilcox, C. (eds.). *The politics of gay rights.* Chicago: University of Chicago Press. pp. 212–213.

21. Largent, S. (1996, July 11). *Congressional Record.* 104th Congress.

22. Barr, R. (1996, July 12). DOMA debate. *Congressional Record.* 104th Congress. p. H7482.

23. Canady, C. (1996, July 12). *Congressional Record.* 104th Congress. p. H7486.

24. Fredriksen, K. (1999, March). Family caregiving responsibilities among lesbians and gay men. *Social Work.* 44(2). p. 146.

25. Kimball, J. (2003, September 24). Homosexuals pose new threat to U.S. border security. Concerned Women for America. Press Release. www.cwfa.org/printerfriendly.asp?id=4629&department=cwa&categoryid=family. Accessed September 29, 2003.

26. *Boston Globe* (1996, September 11).

27. National Gay and Lesbian Task Force Policy Institute (1996). *Capital gains and losses: A state-by-state review of gay-related legislation in 1996.* Washington, DC: Author. www.thetaskforce.org/downloads/cgal96.pdf. Accessed February 5, 2004.

28. National Gay and Lesbian Task Force Policy Institute (1998). *Capital gains and losses: A state by state review of gay, lesbian, bisexual, transgender, and HIV/AIDS-related legislation in 1998.* Washington, DC: Author. p. 13. www.thetaskforce.org/downloads/cgal98.pdf. Accessed February 5, 2004; Missouri's Supreme Court overturned its 1996 anti-gay marriage law in May 1998, but the legislature passed another anti-gay marriage law two years later.

29. Kirchner, L. (2002, October). State court called gay adoption ban "absurd." *Pittsburgh's Out.* p. 3.

30. Cahill, S., Ellen, M., and Tobias, S. (2002). *Family policy: Issues affecting gay, lesbian, bisexual and transgender families.* New York: Policy Institute of the National Gay and Lesbian Task Force. p. 31.

31. H.J. Resolution 56, introduced May 21, 2003.

32. Such challenges have overturned domestic partner policies in Atlanta, GA, Minneapolis, MN, Arlington County, VA, and Massachusetts (all final) as well as Philadelphia (on appeal). Ten other legal challenges were unsuccessful. Source: Gossett, C. (1999, September 4). Dillon goes to court: Legal challenges to local ordinances providing domestic partnership benefits. Paper presented to the annual meeting of the American Political Science Association. Atlanta, GA. Updated in personal communication with Charles Gossett, October 2002.

33. Barillas, C. (1999, July 9). Mass. high court repeals Boston DP ordinance. www.datalounge.com/datalounge/news/record.html?record=4439. Accessed March 8, 2004.

34. WorldNet Daily (2003, August 13). City sued over "domestic partnerships." www.inthedays.com/articles.php?articleId=619. Accessed March 8, 2004.

35. Curtis, C. (2004, March 22). New wording proposed for marriage ban. www.PlanetOut.com. Accessed March 23, 2004.

36. Kennedy, R. (2003). *Interracial intimacies: Sex, marriage, identity, and adoption.* New York: Knopf. Cited in Herbert, B. (2004, March 1). Stolen kisses. *New York Times.*

37. Kristof, N. (2004, March 3). Marriage: Mix and match. *New York Times.*

38. Lewis, R. (2004, March 31). AG sees gay marriage limit. *Boston Globe.*

39. Newton, J. (2004, February 29). Warren Court opened door to wedding chapel for gays; The 1954 ruling against "separate but equal" reverberates today. *Los Angeles Times.*

40. Graff, E. (2004). *What is marriage for? The strange social history of our most intimate institution.* Boston: Beacon Press. p. 156.

41. *Goodridge v. Department of Public Health,* 440 Mass. 309, 321 (2003).

42. Gomes, P. (2004, February 8). For Massachusetts, a chance and a choice. *Boston Globe.* www.boston.com. Accessed February 9, 2004.

43. *The National Catholic Reporter,* the leading voice of liberal Catholicism in the United States, has endorsed the Massachusetts high court's ruling in favor of same-sex marriage, calling it "a beneficial step along the path of human understanding and human rights." An editorial in the lay Catholic weekly noted that the legalization of civil marriage would not affect the Catholic Church's ability to limit marriage to heterosexual couples. It said that "advocating for civil marriage for gays and lesbians is not meant to seem a cavalier defiance of church teaching. The two, for purposes of the current debate, should be separate." Associated Press (2004, February 27). Lay Catholic newspaper endorses court. *New York Blade.* p. 18.

44. General Accounting Office (2004, January 23). Report to Senate Majority Leader William Frist. GAO-04-353R. This represents an increase since 1997, when the GAO issued its first report that listed 1,049 federal laws and benefits that only married spouses can access. General Accounting Office (1997, January 31). Tables of laws in the United States Code involving marital status, by category. www.gao.gov/archive/1997/og97016.pdf. Accessed December 4, 2003.

45. AARP (n.d.). *A woman's guide to pension rights.* Washington, DC: AARP.

CHAPTER 2

1. Green, J. (2000). Antigay: Varieties of opposition to gay rights. In Rimmerman, C., Wald, K., and Wilcox, C. (eds.). *The politics of gay rights.* Chicago: University of Chicago Press. p. 124.

2. Herman, D. (2000). The gay agenda is the devil's agenda: The Christian right's vision and the role of the state. In Rimmerman, C., Wald, K., and Wilcox, C. (eds.). *The politics of gay rights.* Chicago: University of Chicago Press. p. 140. Premillenialists are those who believe that the Bible's Book of Revelations prophesies the end of the world, at which time Christ will come for a second time and rule for 1,000 years. They interpret radical social changes, crises, wars, and natural disasters as evidence of the "end-times."

3. Ibid. p. 98.

4. Hardisty, J. (1999). *Mobilizing resentment: Conservative resurgence from the John Birch Society to the Promise Keepers.* Boston: Beacon Press. p. 103.

5. Berlet, C., and Lyons, M. (2000). *Right-wing populism in America: Too close for comfort.* New York: Guilford Press. p. 235.

6. Hardisty (1999). pp. 120–122.

7. Ibid. p. 121.

8. Connor, K. (2003, April 28). American Renewal. The Legislative Action Arm of the Family Research Council. www.frcaction.org. Accessed November 3, 2003.

9. *Bay Windows* (1997, November 27.)

10. Cahill, S., Cianciotto, J., Colvin, R., Johnson-Lashley, N., and Roberts, F. (2003). *"Marriage Protection Week" sponsors: Are they really interested in "building strong and healthy marriages"?* New York: Policy Institute of the National Gay and Lesbian Task Force. p. 8.

11. Cahill, S. (2004). *Anti-gay groups active in Massachusetts: A closer look.* New York: Policy Institute of the National Gay and Lesbian Task Force. p. 20.

12. Hardisty (1999). p. 105.

13. Focus on the Family (n.d.). State Family Policy Councils. www.family.org/cforum/fpc/. Accessed February 10, 2004.

14. Green, J. (2000). pp. 131–132.

15. Coalition for Marriage (n.d.). Position statements: Homosexual "marriage." www.marriagepreservation.org/position.htm. Accessed January 26, 2004; Coalition members

(2004, January 8). *Boston Globe*. www.boston.com/news/specials/gay_marriage/coalition_marriage/. Accessed January 30, 2004.

16. Sheldon, L. (2003, February). Discrimination and tolerance. *Traditional Values Coalition Report*. 21(1).

17. A 2001 national survey of lesbian, gay, bisexual, and transgender youth by the Gay, Lesbian and Straight Education Network found that 83% had been verbally harassed, 65% sexually harassed, and 42% physically harassed because of their sexual orientation. Kosciw, J., and Cullen, M. (2001). *The GLSEN 2001 national school climate survey: The school-related experiences of our nation's lesbian, gay, bisexual and transgender youth*. New York: Gay, Lesbian and Straight Education Network.

18. Buchanan, P. (n.d.). Mass immigration: Suicide pill of the GOP. www.theamericancause.org/index.htm. Accessed October 3, 2003.

19. People for the American Way (n.d.). Right wing organizations: Traditional Values Coalition. www.pfaw.org/pfaw/general/default.aspx?oid=8992&print=yes. Accessed March 1, 2004; Concerned Women for America. (2002, September 12). Georgia school board ponders creationism. www.cwfa.org/articledisplay.asp?id=2059&department=CWA&categoryid=education. Accessed March 5, 2004; CWA and Eagle Forum are cosponsoring a lobby day in Sacramento, California, March 10, 2004; Concerned Women for America (2004, February 23). Join CWA at the State Capitol! www.cwfa.org/articledisplay.asp?id=5290&department=FIELD&categoryid=misc. Accessed March 5, 2004.

20. People for the American Way (n.d.). Right wing organizations: Family Research Council. www.pfaw.org/pfaw/general/default.aspx?oid=4211&print=yes. Accessed March 1, 2004

21. People for the American Way (n.d.). Right wing organizations: Concerned Women for America. www.pfaw.org/pfaw/general/default.aspx?oid=3151&print=yes. Accessed March 1, 2004. Religious right groups fault public education for promoting secular humanism, and they fault the federal DOE in particular for "a frightening growth in the power of government over people's lives. They denounce the state for using taxes to fund education, usurping parents' roles, supplanting the church as a moral guide, taking God out of America, and using modern educational techniques (seen as experimental psychological manipulation) in place of traditional rote teaching methods." Berlet and Lyons (2000). pp. 210–212.

22. Abraham, Y. (2003, November 18). Transplant targets gay marriage. *Boston Globe*.

23. Maher, B. (n.d.). *Why marriage should be privileged in public policy*. Washington, DC: Family Research Council. www.frc.org/get.cfm?i=IS03D1&v=PRINT. Accessed March 4, 2004.

24. For example, under Arizona's covenant marriage statute, divorce will only be granted in cases of adultery, abandonment, physical or sexual abuse, domestic violence, regular alcohol or drug abuse, the commission of a felony for which a spouse has been sentenced to death or imprisonment, or when both spouses mutually consent to the divorce. Arizona Supreme Court, Administrative Office of the Courts, Court Services Division, Court Programs Unit (2003). Covenant marriage in Arizona. Author. www.supreme.state.az.us/dr/text/covenant. htm. Accessed April 29, 2004.

25. Wilcox, B. (n.d.). Sacred vows, public purposes. Washington, DC: Family Research Council. www.frc.org/get.cfm?i=WT02G2&v=PRINT. Accessed March 4, 2004.

26. Bramlett, M., and Mosher, W. (2002). Cohabitation, marriage, divorce, and remarriage in the United States. National Center for Health Statistics. *Vital Health Stats.* 23(22). p. 28.

27. Mills, R., and Bhandari, S. (2003, September). *Health insurance coverage in the United States: 2002.* Washington, DC: U.S. Census Bureau. www.census.gov/prod/2003pubs/p60-223.pdf. Accessed February 10, 2004.

28. Rennison, C., and Welchans, S. (2000, May). *Special report: Intimate partner violence.* Washington, DC: U.S. Department of Justice, Office of Justice Programs, Bureau of Justice Statistics. Revised January 31, 2002.

29. Web searches were conducted on October 2, 2003. Cahill et al. (2003). pp. 2–3.

30. Coalition for Marriage (n.d.). Position statements: Homosexual "marriage."

31. Sheldon, L. (2003, September 17). Traditional Values Coalition fundraising letter.

32. Gallagher, M. (2003, August 4–11). What marriage is for: Children need mothers and fathers. *Weekly Standard.* 8(45). www.weeklystandard.com. Accessed January 24, 2004.

33. Federal Document Clearinghouse, Inc. (2004, February 25). Bush's remarks on marriage amendment. *New York Times.* p. A18. Santorum, R. (2003, July 9). Americans must preserve institution of marriage. *USA Today.*

34. Belluck, P. (2003, November 14). To avoid divorce, move to Massachusetts. *New York Times,* sect. 4, p. 12.

35. Sprigg, P. (2003). *Question and answer: What's wrong with letting same-sex couples "marry"?* Family Research Council In Focus. Issue No. 256. www.frc.org/get.cfm?i=IF03H01&f=PG03I03. Accessed December 3, 2003.

36. Ibid.

37. Gottman Institute (2001). *12-year study of gay and lesbian couples.* www.gottman.com/research/projects/gaylesbian. Accessed January 5, 2004.

38. Quinn, T. (2001). AIDS in Africa: A retrospective. *Bulletin of the World Health Organization.* 79(12). pp. 1156–1167; Sternberg, S. (2002, November 26). Women now make up half of AIDS cases, UN study finds. *USA Today.* www.usatoday.com/news/health/2002-11-26-aids-usat_x.htm. Accessed April 29, 2004. Sternberg reports that "in the United Kingdom and several European countries, 59% of new HIV cases diagnosed from 1997 to 2001 occurred through heterosexual sex," and that "in the USA, most reported HIV infections among 13- to 19-year-olds were among women and girls, and most of them were infected heterosexually."

39. In fact, while some lesbians are at risk for HIV/AIDS, HIV and AIDS prevalence are much higher among heterosexually active women. The Centers for Disease Control (CDC) notes that "female-to-female transmission of HIV appears to be a rare occurrence." Of the 347 women with AIDS in the U.S. who reported having sex only with women (i.e., lesbians), "98 percent also had another risk—injection drug use in most cases." CDC (n.d.) *HIV/AIDS & U.S. women who have sex with women (WSW).*

40. Sprigg (2003).

41. Massachusetts Family Institute (MFI) (2003, spring). *Issue in focus: Marriage affirmation and protection amendment.* Newton, MA: Author.

42. Regan, M. (2001). *Preserving marriage in an age of counterfeits: How "civil unions" devalue the real thing.* Washington, DC: Family Research Council. p. 17. Cited in MFI (2003, spring).

43. Commonwealth Fund (1999, May). *Health concerns across a woman's lifespan: 1998 survey of women's health.* Cited at Arizona Coalition Against Domestic Violence (n.d.). DV Fact Sheets. Phoenix, AZ: Author. www.azcadv.org/HTML/DV_Facts_Sheets.html.

44. Gay Men's Domestic Violence Project (n.d.). All you want to know . . . Available at www.gmdvp.org/pages/infos.html. Accessed November 5, 2002.

45. Preliminary studies of lesbian couples found that 22% to 46% of lesbians have been in a physically violent same-sex relationship at some point in their lives. Coleman, V. E. (1990). *Confronting lesbian battering.* St. Paul: Minnesota Coalition for Battered Women (46% of lesbians experienced abuse); Brand, P. A., and Kidd, A. H. (1986). Frequency of physical aggression in heterosexual and female homosexual dyads. *Psychological Reports.* 59. pp. 1307–1313 (25% of lesbians reported abuse in past); Lie, G. Schilit, R., Bush, J., Montagne, M., and Reyes, L. (1991). Lesbians in currently aggressive relationships: How frequently do they report aggressive past relationships? *Violence and Victims.* 6.

pp. 121–135 (26% of lesbians reported abuse in current relationship); Kelly, E. E., and Warshafsky, L. (1987). Partner abuse in gay male and lesbian couples. Paper presented at the Third National Conference for Family Violence Researchers. Durham, NH (46% of lesbians and gays used physical aggression with partner); Gay and Lesbian Community Action Council, Minneapolis, MN. (1987). A survey of the twin cities gay and lesbian community: Northstar project (unpublished manuscript) (22% of 900 lesbians had been in a violent relationship). All cited in Renzetti, C., and Miley, C. (eds.) (1996). *Violence in gay and lesbian domestic partnerships*. Binghamton, NY: Harrington Park Press. p. 2.

46. Barnes, P. (1998, February). It's just a quarrel. *American Bar Association Journal*. p. 24. Cited at Arizona Coalition Against Domestic Violence (n.d.). Same-sex DV fact sheet. Phoenix: Author. www.azcadv.org/HTML/SameSexDVfactsheet.html. Accessed February 10, 2004.

47. Rennison, C., and Welchans, S. (2000, May; rev. 2002, January 31). *Intimate partner violence*. Washington, DC: U.S. Department of Justice. Office of Justice Programs.

48. Ash, M, Badgett, M., Folbre, N., Saunders, L., and Albelda, R. (2004, February). *Same-sex couples and their children in Massachusetts: A view from Census 2000*. Amherst, MA: Institute for Gay and Lesbian Strategic Studies.

49. Ash et al. (2004) describing the findings of Florida, R., and Gates, G. (2001, June). *Technology and tolerance: The importance of diversity in high-technology growth*. Washington, DC: Brookings Institution, Center on Urban and Metropolitan Policy. Survey Series.

50. Appelbe, A. (2003, June 13). Canada's "skewed democracy" blamed for homosexual marriage ruling. Christian News Service. www.cnsnews.com. Accessed June 13, 2003.

51. Coalition for Marriage (n.d.). Impact on children. www.marriagepreservation.org/children.htm. Accessed January 26, 2004.

52. Does the relative rise in nonmarital births in the late twentieth century cause poverty in the U.S.? Not necessarily. Studies indicate that public policy toward single-parent families is the more likely culprit. Rates of out-of-wedlock births are higher in several northern European countries, but poverty is much lower. For example, Sweden, Norway, and Denmark have nonmarital birthrates of 47% to 54%. Britain's rate of 34% and France's rate of 37% are also higher than the U.S. rate of 32%. But poverty rates in these countries are much lower. European data for 1995–1996 from *Eurostat Yearbook 1997*; U.S. data for 1998 from *Statistical Abstracts of the United States*, cited in Hirczy de Mino, W. (2000). From bastardy to equality: The rights of nonmarital children and their fathers in comparative perspective. *Journal of Comparative Family Studies*. 31(2). pp. 232–233. A late 1980s study of

poverty differences between single-parent and married-couple families with children found that, in several countries with generous social safety nets, the differences were not significant. In Sweden, 5.5% of single-parent families were poor, versus 5% of married couple families. In the Netherlands the difference was 7.2% versus 7.5%; in France 10% versus 15.8%, and in Britain 16.6% versus 18%. In the U.S., however, the differences were dramatic: 17.9% of married-couple families with children were poor, versus 53.3% of single-parent families with children. This indicates that the poverty gap is not an inevitable state of affairs, but the result of particular public policy choices, which vary from country to country. Poverty is defined as 50% or less of the median income for all households with heads 20 to 55 years old. Katherine McFate (1991). *Poverty, Inequality, and the Crisis of Social Policy: Summary of Findings*. Washington, DC: Joint Center for Political and Economic Studies. p. 32. Cited in Hirczy de Mino (2000). p. 233.

53. Stanton, G. (n.d.). Is marriage in jeopardy? Focus on the Family. http://family. org/cforum/fosi/marriage/FAQs/a0026916.cfm. Accessed October 3, 2003.

54. Abraham, Y. (2003, October 3). O'Malley calls gay marriage a threat; Archbishop opposes definition change. *Boston Globe.* www.boston.com. Accessed October 3, 2003.

55. Congregation for the Doctrine of the Faith (2003, July 31). *Considerations regarding proposals to give legal recognition to unions between homosexual persons.* Vatican City: Author.

56. Stacey, J., and Biblarz, T. (2001). (How) does the sexual orientation of the parent matter? *American Sociological Review.* 66(2). pp. 159–184.

57. Child Welfare League of America (n.d.). Adoption fact sheet. www.cwla.org/ programs/adoption/adoptionfactsheet.htm. Accessed March 1, 2004.

58. Petit, M., and Curtis, P. (1997). Child abuse and neglect: A look at the states. *1997 Child Welfare League of America Stat Book.*

59. Child Welfare League of America (n.d.). Facts and figures. www.cwla.org/ programs/fostercare/factsheet.htm. Accessed March 1, 2004.

60. Eagle, R. (1994). The separation experience of children in long-term care: Theory, resources, and implications for practice. *American Journal of Orthopsychiatry.*

61. Sprigg (2003).

62. Ibid. Other reports include *Dark obsession: The tragedy and threat of the homosexual lifestyle* and *The negative health effects of homosexuality.* All of these reports are authored by Dr. Timothy Dailey.

63. Sheldon, L. (n.d.). Homosexuals recruit public school children: Activists use issues of "safety," "tolerance," and "homophobia" as tactics to promote homosexuality in our nation's schools. *Traditional Values special report.* 18(11).

64. Holmes, W. C., and Slap, G. B. (1998). Sexual abuse of boys: Definitions, prevalence, correlates, sequelae and management. *Journal of the American Medical Association.* 280(21). pp. 1855–1862.

65. Stevenson, M. R. (2000). Public policy, homosexuality and the sexual coercion of children. *Journal of Psychology & Human Sexuality.* 12(4). p. 8.

66. A review of 352 medical records of children evaluated for sexual abuse during a 12-month period at a Denver children's hospital found that less than 1% had been abused by a gay man or a lesbian. Of 269 adult perpetrators of child abuse identified among the 352 cases of abuse, only two were gay or lesbian. The vast majority of the children in the study (82%) "were suspected of being abused by a man or a woman who was, or had been, in a heterosexual relationship with a relative of the child." And the review concluded that in this sample, "a child's risk of being molested by his or her relative's heterosexual partner is over 100 times greater than [the risk of being molested] by someone who might be identifiable as being homosexual, lesbian, or bisexual." Jenny, C., and Roesler, T. A. (1994). Are children at risk for sexual abuse by homosexuals? *Pediatrics.* 94(1). p. 44. In an earlier study of convicted male child molesters in Massachusetts, none of the 175 men were found to have an exclusively homosexual adult sexual orientation or to be primarily attracted to other adult men. Groth, A. N., and Birnbaum, H. J. (1978). Adult sexual orientation and attraction to underage persons. *Archives of Sexual Behavior.* 7(3). pp. 175–181.

67. Stevenson (2000).

68. Ibid.

69. Gearan, A. (2003, June 26). Scalia blasts court on sodomy ruling. Associated Press.

70. Concerned Women of America (CWA) (1996, April). The drive to legalize homosexual "marriage." *Critical Issues Briefing.* p. 1. CWA warned that "Your church could be forced to hire or 'marry' homosexuals" if gay marriage is legalized. Churches that refuse to hire homosexuals "could be closed." In the wake of the Ontario high court ruling in favor of marriage equality for gay couples, CWA again trotted out this canard: "Opponents of same-sex marriage also see the policy as an infringement on religious freedom by forcing churches to marry homosexuals." Appelbe, A. (2003, June 13).

71. Bluey, R. (2003, June 27). Homosexuals push for same-sex marriage after sodomy ruling. Christian News Service.

72. Kimball, J. (2003, September 29). Homosexuals pose new threat to U.S. border security. Concerned Women for America. www.cwfa.org/printerfriendly.asp?id=4629&department= cwa&categoryid=family. Accessed September 29, 2003.

73. Prager, D. (2004, March 2). San Francisco and Islamists: Fighting the same enemy. Posted on the Massachusetts Family Institute website under the heading "Timely Commentary." www.mafamily.org/commentary.htm. Accessed March 5, 2004.

74. Fancher, B., and Parker, J. (2003). Pro-family leaders speak up for "Marriage Protection Week." Agape Press/crosswalk.com. www.crosswalk.com/news/1225015.html. Accessed January 24, 2004.

75. Two days after the September 11, 2001, terrorist attacks, Rev. Jerry Falwell, formerly of the Moral Majority, blamed gays and other groups. In an interview with Rev. Pat Robertson on "The 700 Club," Falwell said, "I really believe that the pagans, and the abortionists, and the feminists, and the gays and the lesbians who are actively trying to make that an alternative lifestyle, the ACLU, People For the American Way, all of them who have tried to secularize America. I point the finger in their face and say, 'you helped this happen.'" Robertson "seemed to agree with Falwell's earlier statements in a prayer during the program," CNN reported. CNN.com (2001, September 14). Falwell apologizes to gays, feminists, lesbians. www.cnn.com/2001/US/09/14/Falwell.apology. Accessed March 1, 2004.

76. McIlhenny, C., McIlhenny, D., and York, F. (1993). *When the wicked seize a city*. LaFayette, LA: Huntington House. p. 232. Cited in Herman (2000). p. 146.

77. Robertson, P., and Slosser, B. (1982). *The secret kingdom*. Nashville: Thomas Nelson. pp. 88–89.

78. Green (2000). p. 124.

79. Battle, J., Cohen, C., Warren, D., Fergerson, G., and Audam, S. (2002). *Say it loud, I'm black and I'm proud: Black Pride Survey 2000*. New York: Policy Institute of the National Gay and Lesbian Task Force and nine Black Pride celebrations. pp. 11, 51. For more on gay people and religion see Comstock, G. (1997). Unrepentant, self-affirming, practicing: Lesbian/bisexual/gay people within organized religion. *Journal for the Scientific Study of Religion*. 36(3). pp. 475–482.

80. Sprigg (2003).

81. Lambda Legal Defense and Education Fund. (2002, February 26). University of Maryland Medical System to be sued Wednesday by gay man prevented from visiting his dying partner at Shock Trauma Center in Baltimore. News Release. Available at www.lambdalegal.org/cgi-bin/iowa/documents/record?record=1011.

82. Emory, T. (2003, November 18). Lesbian couple led fight for landmark ruling. Associated Press. www.boston.com/news/local. Accessed February 9, 2004.

83. Sprigg (2003).

84. LaRue, J. (2004, January 27). Why *Goodridge* is legally and constitutionally wrong. Concerned Women for America Legal Studies. www.cwfa.org/articledisplay.asp?id=5150& department=LEGAL&categoryid=judges. Accessed February 3, 2004.

85. Sprigg (2003).

86. Khan, S. (1998). *Calculated compassion: How the ex-gay movement serves the right's attack on democracy.* Washington, DC: Political Research Associates, National Gay and Lesbian Task Force Policy Institute, and Equal Partners in Faith.

87. Sheldon (2003, September 17).

88. Traditional Values Coalition (n.d.). *Do homosexuals really want the right to marry?* www.traditionalvalues.org. Accessed January 22, 2004. As for polygamy, that issue was decided more than a century ago when it was banned in Utah by the federal government. Concerned Women for America warns that in the wake of *Goodridge*'s injunction that the Massachusetts constitution "forbids the creation of second-class citizens," advocates of group marriage will argue that they are being treated like second-class citizens too: "Polygamists now argue that limiting marriage to two people makes them second-class citizens. Bisexuals can now claim that they are second-class citizens because they cannot obtain fulfillment in marriage unless they're permitted to be married to a man and a woman at the same time." LaRue, J. (2004, January 27).

89. www.marriageprotectionweek.com/mpw_miniposter.pdf. Marriage Protection Week's statement of purpose warned that if gays fail at legalizing group marriage through winning the right of two men or two women to marry, then gays would push for civil unions for three or more people.

90. Knight, R. et al. (2004, January 7). *Marriage: One man, one woman.* Washington, DC: Family Research Council. www.frc.org/get.cfm?i=IF03J01&v=PRINT. Accessed January 15, 2004.

91. Most bisexuals describe themselves as monogamous in their committed relationships, and there is no evidence that bisexuals are any more or less promiscuous than other people. Rust, P. (2001). Two many and not enough: The meanings of bisexual identities. *Journal of Bisexuality.* 31. pp. 57–65.

92. Stanton, G. (n.d.). *How good is* Goodridge? *An analysis of* Goodridge v. Department of Public Health. Colorado Springs, CO: Focus on the Family.

CHAPTER 3

1. U.S. Census Bureau (2001). *Profile of general demographic characteristics: 2000.* Washington, DC: Author. www.census.gov/Press-Release/www/2001/tables/dp_us_2000.pdf.

2. Stacey, J. (2001, July 9). Family values forever: In the Marriage Movement, conservatives and centrists find a home together. *The Nation;* U.S. Census Bureau (2001).

3. Peplau, L. (1993). Lesbian and gay relationships. In Garnets, L., and Kimmel, D. (eds.). *Psychological perspectives on lesbian & gay male experiences.* New York: Columbia University Press; Carrington, C. (1999). *No place like home: Relationships and family life among lesbians and gay men.* Chicago: University of Chicago Press.

4. For studies regarding lesbians, see Herek, G. (2000). Myths about sexual orientation: A lawyer's guide to social science research. *Law and sexuality.* 146(57). He cites a national poll (Results of poll, *San Francisco Examiner*, June 6, 1989) in which 64% of lesbians reported they were in relationships; Bell, A., and Weinberg, M. (1978). *Homosexualities: A study of diversity among men and women.* New York: Simon and Schuster (70–72%); Jay, K., and Young, A. (1977). *The gay report.* New York: Summit Books (80%). For studies regarding gay men, see Herek (2000) (60%); Bell and Weinberg (1978) (51–58%); Jay and Young (1977) (46%). Although these individuals are all considered gay or lesbian in these studies, some would likely identify as bisexual, or are bisexual based on their sexual behavior and/or attraction.

5. Gottman Institute (2001). *12-year study of gay and lesbian couples.* Seattle: Author. www.gottman.com/research/projects/gaylesbian. Accessed January 5, 2004.

6. Bradford, J., Barrett, K., and Honnold, J. (2002). *The 2000 Census and same-sex households: A user's guide.* New York: Policy Institute of the National Gay and Lesbian Task Force. pp. 1–2. Available at www.ngltf.org/pi/census.htm.

7. For a summary of estimates of the gay, lesbian, and bisexual population in the U.S., see Cahill, S., South, K., and Spade, J. (2000). *Outing age: Public policy issues affecting gay, lesbian, bisexual and transgender elders.* New York: Policy Institute of the National Gay and Lesbian Task Force. Available at www.ngltf.org/library. pp. 7–8, 82–83.

8. There were actually 15 states with archaic sex laws on the books in June 2003.

9. Bradford et al. (2002).

10. While 72.4% of heads of household in reporting gay and lesbian couples were non-Hispanic white, 10.5% were black, 11.9% were Hispanic, 2.5% were Asian/Pacific Islander,

0.8% were American Indian, and 1.8% were multiracial. These data were gathered using Table PCT22 of the U.S. Census's American Factfinder, available at http://factfinder. census.gov. For information on how to access these data through the U.S. Census, see Bradford et al. (2002).

11. Patterson, C. J. (1995). Lesbian mothers, gay fathers and their children. In D'Augelli, A. R., and Patterson, C. J. (eds.). *Lesbian, gay and bisexual identities over the lifespan.* New York: Oxford University Press. p. 262. Casper, V., and Schultz, S. B. (1999). *Gay parents/straight schools: Building communication and trust.* New York: Teachers College Press. p. 4.

12. Some individuals in these couples would not identify as gay or lesbian, but by some other term for homosexual. Others would identify as bisexual. Still others would not want to be categorized. But the critical point is that these individuals are in an amorous, long-term, committed, partnered same-sex relationship widely viewed as a "gay or lesbian" relationship. U.S. Census Bureau (2003). *Married-couple and unmarried-partner households: 2000.* Available at www.census.gov/prod/2003pubs/censr-5.pdf.

13. U.S. Census Bureau (2003).

14. Perrin, E. C., and The Committee on Psychosocial Aspects of Child and Family Health (2002). Technical report: Co-parent or second-parent adoption by same-sex parents. *Pediatrics.* 109(2). pp. 341–344.

15. Ferrero, E., Freker, J., and Foster, T. (2002). *Too high a price: The case against restricting gay parenting.* New York: ACLU Lesbian and Gay Rights Project. Available at www. lethimstay.com/pdfs/gayadoptionbook.pdf.

16. Patterson, C. J. (1995). *Lesbian and gay parenting: A resource for psychologists.* Washington, DC: American Psychological Association. Available at www.apa.org/pi/parent. html.

17. Ibid. These conclusions are likely true of bisexual parents as well. Although there is a lack of research focusing specifically on bisexual parents, clearly there are bisexuals in the same-sex couples included in the samples of many of these studies, as well as in many opposite-sex couples. Since many studies do not ask people to self-identify by sexual orientation, there are no conclusive findings on bisexual parents.

18. Stacey, J., and Biblarz, T. (2001). (How) does the sexual orientation of the parent matter? *American Sociological Review.* 66(2). pp. 159–184.

19. Battle, J., Cohen, C., Warren, D., Fergerson, G., and Audam, S. (2002). *Say it loud, I'm black and I'm proud: Black Pride Survey 2000.* New York: Policy Institute of the National Gay and Lesbian Task Force and nine Black Pride celebrations. p. 14.

20. Dang, A., and Frazer, S. (2004). *Black same-sex households in the United States: A report from the 2000 Census.* New York: Policy Institute of the National Gay and Lesbian Task Force and National Black Justice Coalition.

21. Bradford et al. (2002). While only 23% of the white lesbians had given birth to one or more children, 30% of Asian/Pacific Islander lesbians, 43% of Hispanic lesbians, and 60% of black lesbians had biological children.

22. See Badgett, M. V. (2001). *Money, myths and change: The economic lives of lesbians and gay men.* Chicago: University of Chicago Press.

23. Badgett, M. V. (1998). *Income inflation: The myth of affluence among gay men, lesbians, and bisexuals.* New York: Policy Institute of the National Gay and Lesbian Task Force and Institute for Gay and Lesbian Strategic Studies.

24. Human Rights Campaign press releases. HRC and the Urban Institute analyzed data from half a dozen states, including California, Texas, Illinois, New York, and Massachusetts, available in spring 2003. www.hrc.org/newsreleases/2003/census/index.asp. Accessed January 24, 2004.

25. Cahill, S., and Jones, K. (2001). *Leaving our children behind: Welfare reform and the gay, lesbian, bisexual and transgender community.* New York: Policy Institute of the National Gay and Lesbian Task Force.

26. Ibid.

27. D.C. Code Ann. § 16-914(a)(1) ("With respect to matters of custody and visitation . . . sexual orientation, in and of itself, of a party, shall not be a conclusive consideration.").

28. See *J.A.D. v. F.J.D.*, 978 S.W.2d 336 (Mo. 1998) ("A homosexual parent is not ipso facto unfit for custody"); *Tucker v. Tucker*, 910 P.2d 1209 (Utah 1996) (holding that mother's sexual orientation would not by itself disqualify her from being awarded custody); *Bottoms v. Bottoms*, 457 S.E.2d 102 (Va. 1995) (holding that parent's sexual orientation does not by itself render that person unfit to have custody).

29. Tennessee reconsiders ban on gay dad's partner meeting his son. www.gaytoday.com/world/021204wo.asp. Accessed March 2, 2004.

30. Keith, L. (2002, March 28). Lesbian mother in Alabama custody case mulls appeal. Associated Press. *Ex parte H.H. (D.H. v. H.H.),* Ala., No. 1002045 (February 15, 2002).

31. Logue, Patricia M. (2001). *The rights of lesbian and gay parents and their children.* New York: Lambda Legal Defense and Education Fund. Available at www.lambdalegal.org/binary-data/LAMBDA_PDF/pdf/115.pdf.

32. *Rubano v. DiCenzo,* 759 A.2d 959 (RI 2000); *V.C. v. M.J.B.,* 163 N.J. 200, 748 A.2d 539, cert. denied 121 S.Ct. 302 (2000); *S.F. v. M.D.,* 751 A.2d 9 (Md. 2000); *E.N.O. v. L.M.M.,* 429 Mass. 824, 711 N.E.2d 886, cert. denied, 120 S.Ct. 500 (1999); *Holtzman v. Knott,* 195 Wis.2d 649, 533 N.W.2d 419, cert. denied, 116 S.Ct. 475 (1995); *T.B. v. L.R.M.,* 786 A.2d 913 (Pa. 2001).

33. See *In re the Matter of Visitation with C.B.L.,* 723 N.E.2d 316 (Ill. App. Ct. 1999); *In re Thompson,* 11 S.W.3d 913 (Tenn. Ct. App. 1999), appeal denied (Jan. 24, 2000); *Kazmierazak v. Query,* 736 So.2d 106 (Fla. Ct. App. 1999); *Guardianship of Z.C.W. and K.G.W.,* 71 Cal.App.4th 524, 84 Cal.Rptr.2d 48; *Lynda A.H. v. Diane T.O.,* 673 N.Y.S.2d 989 (N.Y. Sup. Ct. 1998).

34. Gay & Lesbian Advocates & Defenders (1999). *Protecting families: Standards for child custody in same-sex relationships.* Boston: Author.

35. Florida, Mississippi, Utah, Arkansas, North Dakota, and Oklahoma limit adoption or foster parenting. Florida bans homosexuals from adopting by law. Its statute reads, "No person eligible to adopt under this statute may adopt if that person is a homosexual." (Fla. Stat. Title VI, Chapter 63, 63.042, 2(d)3.) Mississippi bans same-sex couples from adopting by law. Its statute reads: "Adoption by couples of the same gender is prohibited." (Miss. Code of 1972 as amended, Sec. 93-17-3 (2).) Utah prioritizes heterosexual married couples for placement of foster and adoptive children in state custody by law. Its statute reads, "With regard to children who are in the custody of the state, the division shall establish a policy providing that priority for foster care and adoptive placement shall be provided to families in which both a man and a woman are legally married under the laws of this state." (Title 62A, Ch. 04a, Section 602 (5)(c).) Another Utah statute bans cohabiting unmarried couples from adopting. Utah Code Ann. s. 78-30-1(3) (2004): "(b) A child may not be adopted by a person who is cohabiting in a relationship that is not a legally valid and binding marriage under the laws of this state. For purposes of this Subsection (3) (b), 'cohabiting' means residing with another person and being involved in a sexual relationship with that person." Utah Code Ann. s. 78-30-9 (3) (2004): "(a) The Legislature specifically finds that it is not in a child's best interest to be adopted by a person or persons who are cohabiting in a relationship that is not a legally valid and binding marriage under the laws of this state. Nothing in this section limits or prohibits the court's placement of a child with a single adult who is not cohabiting as defined in Subsection (3)(b). "(b) For purposes of this section, 'cohabiting' means residing with another person and being involved in a sexual relationship with that person." Arkansas bans gays and lesbians from foster parenting, but not from adopting, by regulation. An anti-gay adoption bill was rejected by the Arkansas legislature in 2000. For more information, see www.aclu.org/news/1999/n040699a.html. In spring 2003, North Dakota adopted a law allowing adoption agencies receiving state contracts and licensure to refuse to place children in homes of prospective parents against whom the agencies have religious objections. S. 2188, signed by North Dakota's governor April 23, 2003. Wetzel, D. (2003,

January 29). Senate approves measure to protect religious adoption agencies. Associated Press; Associated Press (2004, May 4). Henry signs measure on gay adoptions.

36. See National Center for Lesbian Rights (2002). Adoption by lesbian, gay and bisexual parents: An overview of current law. Available at www.nclrights.org/publications/adoption. htm; Gay & Lesbian Advocates & Defenders (n.d.). Adoption Issues. Available at www. glad.org/Publications/CivilRightProject/Adopt.pdf; Western PA Freedom to Marry Coalition (1997, August–September). Vermont couples file pro-marriage suit: Freedom to Marry Coalition continue national fight. *Marriage Announcements* (newsletter). Available at www.cs. cmu.edu/afs/cs/user/scotts/ftp/wpaf2mc/newsletter2-4.pdf.

37. National Center for Lesbian Rights (2002, September). Legal recognition of LGBT families. Available at www.nclrights.org/publications/lgbtfamilies.htm#12. *In re Dana*, 660 N.E.2d 397 (N.Y. 1995); *In re Adoption of Two Children by H.N.R.*, 666 A.2d 535 (N.J. Super. Ct. App. Div. 1995); *In re Petition of K.M. and D.M.*, 653 N.E.2d 888 (Ill. App. Ct. 1995); *In re M.M.D. and B.H.M.*, 662 A.2d 837 (D.C. 1995), cited in Gay & Lesbian Advocates & Defenders (n.d.). National Center for Lesbian Rights (2002).

38. An Act Concerning the Best Interest of Children in Adoption Matters, 2000 Conn. Legis. Serv. P.A. 00-228 (S.H.B. 5830) (West) *amending* Conn. Gen. Stat. sec. 45a-724 (1993), cited in Gay & Lesbian Advocates & Defenders (n.d.).

39. Cahill, S., Ellen, M., and Tobias, S. (2002). *Family policy: Issues affecting gay, lesbian, bisexual and transgender families.* New York: Policy Institute of the National Gay and Lesbian Task Force.

40. Shippy, R. A., Cantor, M. H., and Brennan, M. (2001, November). Patterns of support for lesbians and gays as they age. In M. H. Cantor (chair). *Social Support Networks.* Symposium held at the 54th Annual Scientific Meeting of the Gerontological Society of America, Chicago, IL.

41. Wolfe, D. (2000). *Men like us: The GMHC complete guide to gay men's sexual, physical, and emotional well-being.* New York: Ballantine Books. Cited in Dean et al. (2000, January). Lesbian, gay, bisexual, and transgender health: Findings and concerns. *Journal of the Gay and Lesbian Medical Association.* 4(3). pp. 102–151. Shippy, Cantor, and Brennan (2001, November).

42. Liu, G. (1999). Social Security and the treatment of marriage; spousal benefits, earnings sharing and the challenge of reform. *Wisconsin Law Review.* 1. pp. 1–64.

43. Dougherty, T. (2004). *Economic benefits of marriage under federal and Massachusetts law.* New York: Policy Institute of the National Gay and Lesbian Task Force.

44. AARP (n.d.). *Your 401(k) plan: Building toward your retirement security.* Washington, DC: Author.

45. Kaiser Family Foundation (2001). *Inside-OUT: A report on the experiences of lesbians, gays and bisexuals in America and the public's views on issues and policies related to sexual orientation.* Cambridge: Author. www.kff.org/content/2001/3193/LGBSurveyReport.pdf. Accessed August 26, 2003.

46. Dean et al. (2000, January).

47. National Gay and Lesbian Task Force (n.d.). Domestic violence laws in the United States. www.thetaskforce.org/downloads/domesticviolencelawsmap.pdf. Accessed January 3, 2004.

48. Lambda Legal Defense and Education Fund (2002, February 26). University of Maryland Medical System to be sued Wednesday by gay man prevented from visiting his dying partner at shock trauma center in Baltimore. News Release. Available at www.lambdalegal.org/cgi-bin/iowa/documents/record?record=1011.

49. 29 CFR 825.800 § 825.800. Available at www.dol.gov/dol/allcfr/ESA/Title_29/Part_825/29CFR825.800.htm.

50. Jones, Gregg (2002, September 23). Davis to sign bill allowing paid family leave. *Los Angeles Times.*

51. I.R.C. §§ 105, 106.

52. I.R.C. § 152 defines a dependent as an individual who receives half his/her support from the taxpayer and is a member of the taxpayer's residence, which is the dependent's principle place of residence. However, even if a same-sex partner fulfills these two requirements of §152, subsection (b)(5) of the same section requires the taxpayer's relationship to the dependent to be one recognized by local law, thus raising valid concerns about whether a same-sex relationship would qualify.

53. Dougherty (2004).

CHAPTER 4

1. Hardisty, J. (1999). *Mobilizing resentment: Conservative resurgence from the John Birch Society to the Promise Keepers.* Boston: Beacon Press.

2. For more on transgender people and gender identity nondiscrimination laws, see Currah, P., Minter, S., and Green, J. (2000). *Transgender equality: A handbook for activists and policymakers.* New York: Policy Institute of the National Gay and Lesbian Task Force and National Center for Lesbian Rights. Available at www.thetaskforce.org.

3. Vaid, U. (1995). *Virtual equality: The mainstreaming of gay and lesbian liberation.* New York: Anchor Books. p. 112.; Hardisty (1999). p. 98.

4. Shilts, R. (1993). *Conduct unbecoming: Lesbians and gays in the U.S. military—Vietnam to the Persian Gulf.* New York: St. Martin's. Cited in Vaid (1995). pp. 109–110.

5. Ibid.

6. Ibid. p. 115.

7. "Why should Southie vote for Ronald Reagan?" (1980, October 23). *South Boston Marshall.* p. 24.

8. Hardisty, J. (1993, March). Constructing homophobia: Colorado's right-wing attack on homosexuals. *The Public Eye.* Cambridge, MA: Political Research Associates. pp. 1–10.

9. Bull, C., and Gallagher, J. (1996). *Perfect enemies: The religious right, the gay movement, and the politics of the 1990s.* New York: Crown. p. 21.

10. Hardisty (1999). p. 120.

11. Kosovsky Sedgwick, E. (1990). *Epistemology of the closet.* Berkeley: University of California Press. p. 129.

12. Bull and Gallagher (1996). p. 26.

13. Donovan, T., and Bowler, S. (1997). Direct democracy and minority rights: Opinions on anti-gay and lesbian ballot initiatives. In Witt, S., and McCorkle, S. (eds.). *Anti-gay rights: Assessing voter initiatives.* Westport, CT: Praeger. pp. 114–117.

14. Hardisty (1999). p. 106.

15. Vaid (1995). p. 116.

16. Ibid. pp. 119–120.

17. Diamond, S. (1995). *Roads to dominion: Right-wing movements and political power in the United States.* New York: Guilford Press. p. 171. Cited in Shaw, S. (1997). No longer a sleeping giant: The reawakening of religious conservatives in American politics. In Witt, S., and McCorkle, S. (eds.). *Anti-gay rights: Assessing voter initiatives.* Westport, CT: Praeger. p. 15.

18. Donovan, T., and Bowler, S. (1998). Direct democracy and minority rights: An extension. *American Journal of Political Science.* 42. pp. 1020–1024. Cited in Green, J. (2000). Antigay: Varieties of opposition to gay rights. In Rimmerman, C., Wald, K., and Wilcox, C. (eds.). *The politics of gay rights.* Chicago: University of Chicago Press. p. 132.

19. Green (2000). p. 127.

20. Green (2000). p. 133.

21. Fundraising letter reprinted in Political Research Associates (1993). *Constructing homophobia: How the right wing defines lesbians, gay men and bisexuals as a threat to civilization.* Part III. Author. p. 4; Colorado For Family Values (1992). What's wrong with "gay rights"? YOU be the judge! Author. In Political Research Associates (1993).

22. 1990 U.S. Census data on same-sex cohabiting partners; General Social Survey data, late 1980s and early 1990s. Badgett, M. V. (1998). *Income inflation: The myth of affluence among gay men, lesbians, and bisexuals.* New York: Policy Institute of the National Gay and Lesbian Task Force and Institute for Gay and Lesbian Strategic Studies.

23. Goldberg, S. (1995). Civil rights, special rights and our rights. In Berlet, C. (ed.). *Eyes right! Challenging the right wing backlash.* Boston: South End Press. p. 111.

24. Nakagawa, S. (1995). Race, religion, and the right. In Berlet, C. (ed.). *Eyes right! Challenging the right wing backlash.* Boston: South End Press. p. 281.

25. Nakagawa (1995). pp. 280–281.

26. The 2000 Campaign: 2nd presidential debate between Gov. Bush and Vice President Gore (2000, October 12). *New York Times.* p. A22.

27. Press briefing by Ari Fleischer (2003, April 25). www.whitehouse.gov/news/releases/2003/04/20030425-4.html. Accessed July 9, 2003.

28. Levin, D. (1997). The Constitution as rhetorical symbol in western anti-gay rights initiatives: The case of Idaho. In Witt, S., and McCorkle, S. (eds.). *Anti-gay rights: Assessing voter initiatives.* Westport, CT: Praeger. pp. 36–37.

29. Goldberg, S. (1996, Summer). U.S. Supreme Court rules Amendment 2 unconstitutional! *The Lambda Update.* p. 1.

30. National Gay and Lesbian Task Force Policy Institute (2003, November). Populations of jurisdictions with explicitly transgender anti-discrimination laws. www.thetaskforce.org/downloads/TransIncPops.pdf. Accessed February 5, 2004; Currah, P., Minter, S., and Green, J. (2000). *Transgender equality: A handbook for activists and policymakers.* New York: Policy Institute of the National Gay and Lesbian Task Force and National Center for Lesbian Rights.

31. National Gay and Lesbian Task Force (2003, August). GLBT civil rights laws in the U.S. www.thetaskforce.org/downloads/civilrightsmap.pdf. Accessed February 6, 2004.

32. The Human Rights Campaign (HRC) (2003, December). *Statewide anti-discrimination laws and policies.* www.hrc.org/Template.cfm?Section=Your_Community& Template=/ContentManagement/ContentDisplay.cfm&ContentID=13381. Accessed February 5, 2004.

33. Rayside, D. (2002). Recognizing same-sex relationships: Profiling change in Canada and the United States. Paper delivered at the annual meeting of the American Political Science Association, August 29–September 1, 2002, Boston, MA, pp. 21–23; Human Rights Campaign (2002). *Domestic partner benefits.* www.hrc.org/worknet/dp/index.asp. Accessed December 4, 2003; NGLTF Policy Institute internal analysis.

34. Human Rights Campaign (2002).

35. 79% of Americans favor the right of openly lesbian, gay, and bisexual people to serve in the United States Armed Forces, according to a 2003 CNN/*USA Today*/Gallup poll. Source: Center for the Study of Sexual Minorities in the Military (CSSMM) (2003, December 23). 79% of public now favors allowing gays to serve openly. Author. www.gaymilitary.ucsb.edu/PressCenter/press_rel_2003_1223.htm#. Accessed January 8, 2004. A 2001 poll found a majority of Americans (56% to 38%) supported allowing openly gay and lesbian people to serve in the military. Kaiser Family Foundation (2001). *Inside-OUT: A report on the experiences of lesbians, gays and bisexuals in America and the public's views on issues and policies related to sexual orientation.* Cambridge: Author. www.kff.org/content/ 2001/3193/LGBSurveyReport.pdf. Accessed August 26, 2003.

36. Yang, A. (2001). *The National Election Study and gay and lesbian rights: Support for equality grows.* New York: Policy Institute of the National Gay and Lesbian Task Force; Yang, A. (1999). *From wrongs to rights, 1973–1999: Public opinion on gay and lesbian Americans moves toward equality.* New York: Policy Institute of the National Gay and Lesbian Task Force.

37. Yang (2001).

38. Newport, F. (2003, May 15). Six out of 10 Americans say homosexual relations should be recognized as legal; But Americans are evenly divided on issue of legal civil unions between homosexuals giving them legal rights of married couples. Gallup News Service.

39. 96% of parents. Kaiser Family Foundation (2001).

40. Kaiser Family Foundation (2001).

41. Merkle, D. (2002, April 2). More Americans support gay adoption. ABCNews.com. http://abcnews.go.com/sections/us/DailyNews/gayadopt_poll020402.html. Accessed November 12, 2002.

42. Newport (2003, May 15).

43. Kaiser Family Foundation (2001); Yang (2001). Sherrill, K. (2004). *Same-sex marriage, civil unions, and the 2004 presidential election.* New York: Policy Institute of the National Gay and Lesbian Task Force.

44. Openly gay, lesbian, and bisexual voters were 5.0% of all voters in the 1996 Congressional/Presidential election, 4.2% in 1998, and 4.1% in 2000, according to Voter News Service national exit polls. Bailey, R. (2000). *Out and voting II: The gay, lesbian, and bisexual vote in congressional elections, 1990–1998.* New York: Policy Institute of the National Gay and Lesbian Task Force; unpublished analysis of 2000 VNS data.

45. In 1998, 89% of African American voters voted Democratic, as did 79% of Jewish voters, and 67% of gay, lesbian, and bisexual voters. Bailey (2000); unpublished analysis of 2000 Voter News Service exit poll data.

46. This estimate derives from the following data: *openly* gay, lesbian, and bisexual voters are 4–5% of all voters, and the overwhelming majority vote Democratic. Assuming the 4–5% figure represents an undercount, as some gay people may not want to "out" themselves on an exit poll, and given that two-thirds to three-quarters of gay people vote Democratic, the percentage of Democratic primary voters who are gay, lesbian, or bisexual is likely close to 10%. Sources within the Democratic National Committee make a similar estimate.

47. Bull and Gallagher (1996). p. 32.

48. Although mainstream media generally refer to right wing party activists as conservative, some are more accurately described as reactionary, since they seek to repeal many of the changes implemented under the Great Society and civil rights reforms of the 1960s and early 1970s, and in many cases even aspects of the New Deal of the 1930s. Many promote a breaking down of church–state separation, as well as the repeal of many environmental regulations of business promoted by the Nixon Administration.

49. Bull and Gallagher (1996). p. 68.

50. Ibid. p. 79.

51. A 1992 National Gay and Lesbian Task Force report faulted Governor Clinton for signing a law requiring that people with HIV be reported to state health authorities, and for not supporting legislative efforts in 1991 to repeal Arkansas' gay-only sodomy law. It also reported that Clinton had "flip-flopped" on whether or not he supported a federal sexual orientation nondiscrimination law.

52. Bull and Gallagher (1996). pp. 74–78.

53. Ibid. pp. 91–92.

54. Ibid. p. 94.

55. Berlet, C., and Margaret, Q. (1995). Theocracy and white supremacy: Behind the culture war to restore traditional values. In Berlet, C. (ed.). *Eyes right! Challenging the right wing backlash.* Boston: South End Press. p. 15.

56. Bull and Gallagher (1996). p. 94.

57. Ibid. p. 129.

58. Rhoads, H. (1993, March). Cruel crusade: The holy war against lesbians and gays. *The Progressive.* 53:7. p. 18; Bull and Gallagher (1996). p. 95; Bailey (2000).

59. *Baker v. Nelson,* 191 N.W.2d 185 (Minn. 1971).

60. *Baehr v. Lewin,* 852 P.2d 44 (Haw. 1993) (plurality).

61. *Baehr v. Miike,* CIV No. 91-1394, 1996 WL 694235 (Haw. Cir. Ct. Dec. 3, 1996).

62. Ibid.

63. As cited in the *Boston Globe* (1996, April 14).

64. Ibid.

65. Significantly, Governor George W. Bush and Senator John McCain did not sign on, though Bush's spokesperson said this was because Bush had a policy against signing pledges. *Des Moines Register* (1999, August 13).

66. Sandalow, M. (1999, November 9). McCain welcomes support of gays in GOP; Candidate meets with Log Cabin group. *San Francisco Chronicle.*

67. Ramer, H. (1999, December 27). Bauer: Gay marriage is worse than terrorism. Associated Press.

68. Keen, L. (1999, October 15). An about face for Bush? Opinion on appointing gays remains murky. *Washington Blade.*

69. *The Advocate* (2000, July 18). A sodomy law's last stand. Originally quoted by Elliot, D. (1994, January 22). *Austin-American Statesman.*

70. Cahill, S., and Ludwig, E. (1999). *Courting the vote: The 2000 presidential candidates on gay, lesbian, bisexual and transgender issues.* New York: Policy Institute of the National Gay

and Lesbian Task Force.

71. National Gay and Lesbian Task Force (n.d.). Election center 2000: VP candidate profile Richard "Dick" Cheney. www.ngltf.org/elections/cheney.htm. Accessed January 8, 2004.

72. This statement supports a number of anti-gay policies, including denying health care benefits to domestic partners, the reduction of HIV/AIDS services, the promotion of "abstinence-only-until-marriage" as the only form of STD and pregnancy prevention, which does not apply to same-sex couples because they can not get married, and the continued censorship of homosexuality in the curricula of public schools.

73. Republican National Committee (2000). *Platform 2000: Renewing America's purpose together*. www.rnc.org/gopinfo/platform. Accessed July 2, 2003.

74. Democratic National Committee (2000). *The 2000 Democratic National Platform: Prosperity, progress, and peace*. www.democrats.org/about/platform.html. Accessed July 2, 2003.

75. Marriage Protection Week, 2003, by the President of the United States of America: A proclamation. (2003, October 3). www.whitehouse.gov/news/releases/2003/10/print/2003 1003-12.html. Accessed January 13, 2004.

76. City News Service (2004, January 8). Gay church group announces national "Freedom to Marry Week" actions. Author.

77. Washington, W. (2004, April 1). White House, counsel split on gay rights; Official had questioned antidiscrimination law. *Boston Globe*.

78. Slater, W. (1999, March 23). Bush opposes adoption by gays. *Dallas Morning News*.

79. Zeller, T. (2004, January 18). Two fronts: Promoting marriage, fighting poverty. *New York Times*. p. WK3.

80. Press briefing by Ari Fleischer (2003, April 25). www.whitehouse.gov/news/releases/ 2003/04/20030425-4.html. Accessed July 9, 2003; The 2000 Campaign; 2nd presidential debate between Gov. Bush and Vice President Gore (2000, October 12).

81. Slater (1999, March 23); Burka, P. (1999, September). James Byrd, Jr.: Law's latest symbol. *Texas Monthly*. www.texasmonthly.com/mag/1999/sep/byrd.php. Accessed July 9, 2003.

82. Connolly C. (1999, December 15). Gore's views on gays in military get public voice. *Washington Post*. p. A6; Excerpts from debate among G.O.P candidates (2000, January 7). *New York Times*. p. A15.

83. Kaiser Family Foundation (2003, March 24). Daily HIV/AIDS report. www.kaiser network.org/daily_reports/rep_index.cfm?hint=1&DR_ID=16743. Accessed July 9, 2003.

84. For example, see Bybee, J. S., *The Equal Protection Clause: A note on the (non)relationship between* Romer v. Evans *and* Hunter v. Erickson, 6 Wm. & Mary Bill Rts. J. 201, 224 (1997); Tymkovich, T. M., Dailey, J. D., and Farley, P., *Gay rights and the courts: The Amendment 2 controversy: A tale of three theories: Reason and prejudice in the battle over Amendment 2,* 68 U. Colo. L. Rev. 287 (1997); Among Bush's anti-gay cabinet members are Attorney General John Ashcroft, who opposed James Hormel's nomination to become Ambassador to Luxembourg because Hormel is gay, and Interior Secretary Gail Norton, who invited discredited psychologist Paul Cameron to testify in support of Colorado's anti-gay Amendment 2, which was found unconstitutional by the U.S. Supreme Court in *Romer v. Evans,* 1996.

85. Towery, J. (n.d.). *Protecting the civil rights and religious liberty of faith-based organizations: Why religious hiring rights must be preserved.* Washington, DC: White House Office of Faith-Based and Community Initiatives. www.whitehouse.gov/government/fbci/ booklet.pdf. Accessed January 6, 2004.

86. Russell, S. (2003, June 14). Funds for S.F. AIDS program in peril; CDC threatens to pull money for "obscene" campaign. *San Francisco Chronicle.* p. A1.

87. Kaiser, J. (2003). Politics and biomedicine: Studies of gay men, prostitutes come under scrutiny. *Science.* pp. 300–403; Politicizing science (2003, June 9). *Bangor Daily News.* p. A8.

88. Radow, J. (2003, October 28). Researcher "hit list" undermines NIH peer-review process, charges Rep. Waxman. *Washington Fax;* Herbert, B. (2003, November 3). The big chill at the lab. *New York Times.* p. A19. As NIH Director Elias A. Zerhouni, M.D., pointed out, some of these studies examine male sexual dysfunction and impotence, which is a major cause of marital relationship dissatisfaction and divorce. The Traditional Values Coalition is opposing research that could help solve sexual dysfunction, which is a major source of familial stress and dissolution.

89. Anderson, N. (2003, July 3). Candidates leery of gay marriage debate. *Los Angeles Times.* www.latimes.com/news/nationworld/politics/la-na-marriage3jul03001429,0,2329538. story?coll=la-news-politics-national. Accessed July 9, 2003.

90. President Bush discusses top priorities for the U.S. (2003, July 30). www.whitehouse. gov/news/releases/2003/07/20030730-1.html. Accessed July 31, 2003.

91. Bush, G. W. (2003, November 18). President defends the sanctity of marriage: Statement by the President. www.whitehouse.gov/news/releases/2003/11/20031118-4.html. Accessed December 17, 2003.

92. Jones, S. (2004, January 21). Bush's comments on marriage draw praise, criticism. Cybercast News Service. www.CNSNews.com. Accessed January 21, 2004.

93. Dobbin, M. (2004, February 6). Enraged foes of gay marriage gear up for fight; Massachusetts ruling energizes drive for a constitutional ban on same-sex wedlock. *Sacramento Bee.*

94. Washington, W. (2004, February 19). Bush "troubled" by gay marriage, but is quiet on amendment plans. *Boston Globe.*

95. Mitchell, A. (2000, April 14). Bush talks to gays and calls it beneficial. *New York Times.* p. A26.

96. Domestic Partners Benefits and Obligations Act, H.R. 638, 107th Cong. (2003).

97. Press briefing by Scott McClellan (2003, July 30). www.whitehouse.gov/news/releases/2003/07/20030731-9.html. Accessed August 1, 2003.

98. Mychal Judge Police and Fire Chaplains Public Safety Officers' Benefit Act of 2002, Pub. L. No. 107-196, 116 Stat. 719. Codified at 42 U.S.C. § 3796 (2002).

99. Becker, Susan J. (2003). Tumbling towers as turning points: Will 9/11 usher in a new civil rights era for gay men and lesbians in the United States? *William & Mary Journal of Women and Law.* 9. pp. 207–253.

100. Kornblut, A. (2004, January 21). Bush demonstrates willingness to tackle divisive cultural issues. *Boston Globe.*

101. The White House, Office of the Press Secretary (2004, February 24). Remarks by the President.

102. Mason, J. (2003, November 19). Texans urge ban on gay unions. *Houston Chronicle.*

103. Fancher, B., and Parker, J. (2003). Pro-family leaders speak up for "Marriage Protection Week." Agape Press/crosswalk.com. www.crosswalk.com/news/1225015.html. Accessed January 24, 2004.

104. Farah, J. (2003, July 7). Impeach the "Sodomy 6." www.worldnetdaily.com/news/article.asp?ARTICLE-ID=33447. Accessed January 24, 2004.

105. Catholic Action League (2003, November 18). Catholic Action League condemns SJC decision on same-sex marriage. www.frmcgivneyassembly.org/CatholicActionLeague.html.

106. Traditional Values Coalition special report (n.d.). *Judges: Our robed masters; A call to end judicial tyranny!* www.traditionalvalues.org. Accessed January 22, 2004.

107. Madison, J. (1987). Federalist 10. *The Federalist Papers*. New York: Penguin Classics.

108. Federal Document Clearinghouse, Inc. (2004, February 25). Bush's remarks on marriage amendment. *New York Times*. p. A18.

109. Alliance for Marriage (n.d.). Multicultural coalition reintroduces federal marriage amendment in Congress: Strong bipartisan sponsorship reflects the fact that the future of marriage in America is more important than partisan politics. www.allianceformarriage. org/reports/fma/fma.cfm. Accessed March 2, 2004.

110. Barillas, C. (1999, July 9). Mass. high court repeals Boston DP ordinance. Available at www.datalounge.com/datalounge/news/record.html?record=4439. Loven, J. (2004, February 29). Congress not rushing gay marriage ban. Associated Press.

111. City sued over "domestic partnerships" (2003, August 13). www.inthedays.com/ articles.php?articleId=619.

112. Federal Document Clearinghouse, Inc. (2004, February 25).

113. Bush speech stirs marriage debate among Republicans. *The Advocate*. www.advocate. com/new_news.asp?ID=11063&sd=01/23/04. Accessed March 1, 2004.

114. Boswell, J. (1995). *Same-sex unions in premodern Europe*. New York: Vintage Books.

115. Graff, E. (2004). *What is marriage for? The strange social history of our most intimate institution*. Boston: Beacon Press.

116. Grossman, R. (2004, February 29). A perfect union? Marriage has seen many makeovers. The push to allow gays to wed is just the latest of many social forces that have reshaped matrimony. *Chicago Tribune*.

117. Ibid.

118. Ibid.

119. Ibid.

120. Aristotle (1982). *The politics*. New York: Penguin Classics. Book II, Part 9; Siculus, D. (1992). *Volume 11, Fragments of books 21–32*. Library of History (Loeb Classical Library). Cambridge, MA: Harvard University Press.

121. Norris, Senator D. (1993) Criminal law (sexual offences) bill 1993; Second stage speech, Tuesday 29 June 1993, Seanad Eireann (Irish Senate). Reprinted in Collins, E., and O'Carroll, I. (1995). *Lesbian and gay visions of Ireland: Towards the twenty-first century*. London: Cassell. p. 17.

122. Burress, C. (2004, February 27). Scientists counter Bush view; Families varied, say anthropologists. *San Francisco Chronicle.* These are all direct quotes except the last one about berdaches, which is a paraphrase but directly quoted from the news article. Berdaches were biological males who were viewed as embodying a third sex that had both male and female components.

123. Cahill, S., Hernandez, J., Hill, R., and Varghese, M. (2003). *The 2004 Democratic presidential candidates on gay, lesbian, bisexual, and transgender issues.* New York: Policy Institute of the National Gay and Lesbian Task Force; National Gay and Lesbian Task Force (2004, January). The presidential candidates' positions on LGBT issues. New York: Policy Institute of the National Gay and Lesbian Task Force. www.ngltf.org/electioncenter/ SummaryComparison.pdf. Accessed January 30, 2004.

124. Dang, A. (2004). *The Democratic presidential candidates on marriage equality for same-sex couples.* New York: Policy Institute of the National Gay and Lesbian Task Force. www.ngltf.org/electioncenter/DemsMarriage.pdf. Accessed January 30, 2004.

125. National Gay and Lesbian Task Force (2004, February). Marriage map. www.ngltf.org/downloads/marriagemap.pdf; Adoption and foster care map. www.ngltf.org/ downloads/adoptionmap.pdf. Accessed February 9, 2004; Associated Press (2004, May 4). Henry signs measure on gay adoptions.

126. Cianciotto, J., and Cahill, S. (2003). *Education policy issues affecting lesbian, gay, bisexual and transgender youth.* New York: Policy Institute of the National Gay and Lesbian Task Force. p. 50.

127. Forster, S. (2004, March 13). Marriage amendment sets stage for battle; Clearing Senate, proposal is expected to be target in November elections. *Milwaukee Journal-Sentinel.*

CHAPTER 5

1. General Accounting Office (2004, January 23). Report to Senate Majority Leader William Frist. GAO-04-353R. This represents an increase since 1997, when the GAO issued its first report that listed 1,049 federal laws and benefits that only married spouses can access. General Accounting Office (1997, January 31). *Tables of laws in the United States Code involving marital status, by category.* www.gao.gov/archive/1997/og97016.pdf. Accessed December 4, 2003

2. Adapted from a profile of Mickie Mashburn and Lois Marrero in Cahill, S., Ellen, M., and Tobias, S. (2002). *Family policy: Issues affecting gay, lesbian, bisexual and transgender families.* New York: Policy Institute of the National Gay and Lesbian Task Force. pp. 152–153.

3. Adapted from a speech given by Larry Courtney at the National Gay and Lesbian Task Force Leadership Awards Deck Party, in Provincetown, Massachusetts, August 25, 2002.

4. Dahir, M. (2003, March 4). A federal nod to gay partners: Will Peggy Neff's award from the federal Victim Compensation Fund help all same-sex couples win more legal recognition? *The Advocate.*

5. Johnson, J. (2001, October 22). Homosexuals seek survivor benefits intended for families. Cybercast News Service (CNSNews.com.). www.dadi.org/homogred.htm. Accessed February 9, 2004. Knight's use of the term *hijack* was particularly offensive in that he was describing efforts of gay partners to get help dealing with the grief of losing their loved ones in terrorist attacks caused by the hijacking of four jet aircraft.

6. Concerned Women for America, quoted in People for the American Way Foundation (PFAWF) (2002). *Hostile climate: Report on anti-gay activity.* 8th edition. Washington, DC: Author. p. 33.

7. The Culture and Family Institute of Concerned Women for America quoted in PFAWF (2002). p. 31.

8. Dobson, J. (2002, January). Dr. Dobson's newsletter. Colorado Springs, CO: Focus on the Family. www.family.org/docstudy/newsletters/a0019238.html. Accessed February 9, 2004.

9. Focus on the Family, quoted in PFAWF (2002). p. 31.

10. Sheldon, quoted in PFAWF (2002). p. 33; Berkowitz, B. (2001, October 21). Religious right on the ropes. AlterNet. www.alternet.org/print.html?StoryID=11840. Accessed February 9, 2004.

11. Sheldon, quoted in PFAWF (2002). p. 33.

12. Sprigg, quoted in PFAWF (2002). p. 33.

13. PFAWF (2002). pp. 31–32.

14. Human Rights Campaign (2001). *The state of the workplace for lesbian, gay, bisexual and transgender Americans 2001.* Washington, DC: Author; Human Rights Campaign (2002). *Domestic partner benefits.* Washington, DC: Author. www.hrc.org/worknet/dp/index.asp. Accessed November 2, 2002.

15. Levene, Abigail (2001, April 1). World's first legal gay weddings held in Amsterdam. *Reuters.* www.travelandtranscendence.com/holland-news.html. Accessed December 4, 2003;

Associated Press (2003, January 30). Belgium approves same-sex marriages. CBS.com. www.cbsnews.com/stories/2003/01/30/world/main538668.shtml. Accessed December 4, 2003.

16. Rohter, Larry (2000, June 10). Brazil grants some legal recognition to same-sex couples. *New York Times*; Hacker, Peter (2002, September 25). Taiwan move to allow gay unions. *BBC News*; Hogg, Chris (2003, October 28). Retrieved December 4, 2003, from http://news.bbc.co.uk/2/hi/asia-pacific/3219721.stm; Australian state grants partner rights. www.365Gay.com. Accessed December 4, 2003.

17. An October 2003 Decision Research poll found 59% support same-sex marriage rights, while three-quarters would accept a court ruling in favor of gay marriage. Decision Research (2003, October 29). www.ftmmass.org/PollMemoOct2911.pdf. Accessed January 5, 2004; A November 2003 *Boston Globe*/WBZ TV poll found 50% in favor of marriage for same-sex couples, 38% opposed, and 11% undecided. Phillips, F., and Klein, R. (2003, November 23). 50% in poll back SJC ruling on gay marriage. *Boston Globe*. p. A1.

18. New Jersey voters favored same-sex marriage in a July 2003 Zogby poll 55% to 41%. Peterson, I. (2003, July 29). Metro briefing New Jersey: Poll finds support for gay marriage. *New York Times*; Decision Research memorandum (2003, November 18). 57% to 38% of Connecticut voters favor civil marriage for same-sex couples. www.lmfct.org. Accessed December 4, 2003; 54% of New Hampshire voters favor same-sex marriage in May 2003 University of New Hampshire poll; Staff Writer (2003, May 23). New Hampshire residents favoring law for same-sex marriages. Associated Press.

19. *Wall Street Journal*/NBC News poll conducted by Peter Hart and Robert Teeter, September 9–13, 1999. Cited in Lambda Legal Defense and Education Fund (1999, December 10). Preliminary notes on the Hawaii Supreme Court's 12/9/99 decision. www.lambdalegal.org/cgi-bin/iowa/documents/record?record=544. Accessed December 4, 2003.

20. 2001–2002 Freshmen survey: Their opinions, activities, and goals (2002, February 1). *Chronicle of Higher Education*. p. A37. www.chronicle.com/free/v48/i21/opinions.htm. Accessed December 4, 2003.

21. Seelye, K. Q., and Elder, J. (2003, December 21). Strong support is found for ban on gay marriage. *New York Times*. p. A1; Grossman, C. (2003, October 7). Public opinion is divided on gay marriages. *USA Today*; ABC News Poll (2003, September 22). Most oppose homosexual marriage, but don't want to amend constitution. Retrieved January 8, 2004, from http://abcnews.go.com/images/pdf/883a33GayMarriage.pdf. While some polls found a slight majority in favor of the amendment, others found more Americans opposed to the

Federal Marriage Amendment than for it. For example, a Sacred Heart University Polling Institute poll found 47% opposed and 42% in favor. Sacred Heart University Polling Institute (2004, March). Sacred Heart University poll: Political and social issues 2004. Bridgeport, CT: Author.

22. Pew Research Center for the People and the Press (2004, February 27). Gay marriage a voting issue, but most likely for opponents: Constitutional amendment rates as a low priority. Author. Retrieved March 1, 2004 from http://people-press.org/reports/display.php3?ReportID=204.

Select Bibliography

Aristotle (1982). *The politics.* New York: Penguin Classics.

Ash, M., Badgett, M., Folbre, N., Saunders, L., and Albelda, R. (2004, February). *Same-sex couples and their children in Massachusetts: A view from Census 2000.* Amherst, MA: Institute for Gay and Lesbian Strategic Studies.

Badgett, M. V. (1998). *Income inflation: The myth of affluence among gay men, lesbians, and bisexuals.* New York: Policy Institute of the National Gay and Lesbian Task Force and Institute for Gay and Lesbian Strategic Studies.

Battle, J., Cohen, C., Warren, D., Fergerson, G., and Audam, S. (2002). *Say it loud, I'm black and I'm proud: Black Pride Survey 2000.* New York: Policy Institute of the National Gay and Lesbian Task Force and nine Black Pride celebrations.

Becker, Susan J. (2003). Tumbling towers as turning points: Will 9/11 usher in a new civil rights era for gay men and lesbians in the United States? *William & Mary Journal of Women and Law.* 9. pp. 207–253.

Berlet, C., and Lyons, M. (2000). *Right-wing populism in America: Too close for comfort.* New York: Guilford Press.

Boswell, J. (1995). *Same-sex unions in premodern Europe.* New York: Vintage Books.

Bramlett, M., and Mosher, W. (2002). Cohabitation, marriage, divorce, and remarriage in the United States. *Vital Health Stats.* 23(22). p. 28.

Bull, C., and Gallagher, J. (1996). *Perfect enemies: The religious right, the gay movement, and the politics of the 1990s.* New York: Crown.

Cahill, S. (2004). *Anti-gay groups active in Massachusetts: A closer look.* New York: Policy Institute of the National Gay and Lesbian Task Force.

Cahill, S., Cianciotto, J., Colvin, R., Johnson-Lashley, N., and Roberts, F. (2003). *"Marriage Protection Week" sponsors: Are they really interested in "building strong and healthy marriages"?* New York: Policy Institute of the National Gay and Lesbian Task Force.

Cahill, S., Hernandez, J., Hill, R., and Varghese, M. (2003). *The 2004 Democratic presidential candidates on gay, lesbian, bisexual, and transgender issues.* New York: Policy Institute of the National Gay and Lesbian Task Force.

Cahill, S., Ellen, M., and Tobias, S. (2002). *Family policy: Issues affecting gay, lesbian, bisexual and transgender families.* New York: Policy Institute of the National Gay and Lesbian Task Force. www.ngltf.org/library.

Cahill, S., and Jones, K. (2001). *Leaving our children behind: Welfare reform and the gay, lesbian, bisexual and transgender community.* New York: Policy Institute of the National Gay and Lesbian Task Force.

Cahill, S., South, K., and Spade, J. (2000). *Outing age: Public policy issues affecting gay, lesbian, bisexual and transgender elders.* New York: Policy Institute of the National Gay and Lesbian Task Force. www.ngltf.org/library.

Cahill, S., and Ludwig, E. (1999). *Courting the vote: The 2000 presidential candidates on gay, lesbian, bisexual and transgender issues.* New York: Policy Institute of the National Gay and Lesbian Task Force.

Centers for Disease Control (n.d.). *HIV/AIDS & U.S. women who have sex with women (WSW).* Atlanta: Author.

Cianciotto, J., and Cahill, S. (2003). *Education policy issues affecting lesbian, gay, bisexual and transgender youth.* New York: Policy Institute of the National Gay and Lesbian Task Force.

Collins, E., and O'Carroll, I. (1995). *Lesbian and gay visions of Ireland: Towards the twenty-first century.* London: Cassell.

Currah, P., Minter, S., and Green, J. (2000). *Transgender equality: A handbook for activists and policymakers.* New York: Policy Institute of the National Gay and Lesbian Task Force and National Center for Lesbian Rights. www.thetaskforce.org.

Dang, A. (2004). *The Democratic presidential candidates on marriage equality for same-sex couples.* New York: Policy Institute of the NGLTF. www.ngltf.org/electioncenter/DemsMarriage.pdf.

Dang, A., and Frazer, S. (2004). *Black same-sex households in the United States: A report from the 2000 Census.* New York: Policy Institute of the National Gay and Lesbian Task Force and National Black Justice Coalition.

Dean, L., et al. (2000, January). Lesbian, gay, bisexual, and transgender health: Findings and concerns. *Journal of the Gay and Lesbian Medical Association.* 4(3). pp. 102–151. www.glma.org/pub/jglma/vol4/3/j43text.pdf.

Democratic National Committee (2000). *The 2000 Democratic National Platform: Prosperity, progress, and peace.* www.democrats.org/about/platform.html.

Donovan, T., and Bowler, S. (1997). Direct democracy and minority rights: Opinions on anti-gay and lesbian ballot initiatives. In Witt, S., and McCorkle, S. (eds.). *Anti-gay rights: Assessing voter initiatives.* Westport, CT: Praeger. pp. 107–125.

Dougherty, T. (2004). *Economic benefits of marriage under federal and Massachusetts law.* New York: Policy Institute of the National Gay and Lesbian Task Force.

Gallagher, M. (2003, August 4–11). What marriage is for: Children need mothers and fathers. *The Weekly Standard.* 8(45).

Gay & Lesbian Advocates & Defenders (1999). *Protecting families: Standards for child custody in same-sex relationships.* Boston: Author.

General Accounting Office (2004, January 23). Report to Senate Majority Leader William Frist. GAO-04-353R.

General Accounting Office (1997, January 31). Tables of laws in the United States Code involving marital status, by category. www.gao.gov/archive/1997/og97016.pdf

Goldberg, S. (1995). Civil rights, special rights and our rights. In Berlet, C. (ed.). *Eyes right! Challenging the right wing backlash.* Boston: South End Press. pp. 109–112.

Gottman Institute (2001). *12-year study of gay and lesbian couples.* Seattle: Author.

Graff, E. (2004). *What is marriage for? The strange social history of our most intimate institution.* Boston: Beacon Press.

Green, J. (2000). Antigay: Varieties of opposition to gay rights. In Rimmerman, C., Wald, K., and Wilcox, C. (eds.) *The politics of gay rights.* Chicago: University of Chicago Press. pp. 121–138.

Groth, A. N., and Birnbaum, H. J. (1978). Adult sexual orientation and attraction to underage persons. *Archives of Sexual Behavior.* 7(3). pp. 175–181.

Hardisty, J. (1999). *Mobilizing resentment: Conservative resurgence from the John Birch Society to the Promise Keepers.* Boston: Beacon Press.

Hardisty, J. (1993, March). Constructing homophobia: Colorado's right-wing attack on homosexuals. *The Public Eye.* Cambridge, MA: Political Research Associates. pp. 1–10.

Herman, D. (2000). The gay agenda is the devil's agenda: The Christian right's vision and the role of the state. In Rimmerman, C., Wald, K., and Wilcox, C. (eds.) *The politics of gay rights.* Chicago: University of Chicago Press. pp. 139–160.

Holmes, W. C., and Slap, G. B. (1998). Sexual abuse of boys: Definitions, prevalence, correlates, sequelae and management. *Journal of the American Medical Association.* 280(21). pp. 1855–1862.

Human Rights Campaign (2002). *Domestic partner benefits.* Washington, DC: Author.

Human Rights Campaign (2001). *The state of the workplace for lesbian, gay, bisexual and transgender Americans 2001.* Washington, DC: Author.

Jenny, C., and Roesler, T. A. (1994). Are children at risk for sexual abuse by homosexuals? *Pediatrics.* 94(1). pp. 41–44.

Kennedy, R. (2003). *Interracial intimacies: Sex, marriage, identity, and adoption.* New York: Knopf Publishing Group.

Khan, S. (1998). *Calculated compassion: How the ex-gay movement serves the right's attack on democracy.* Washington, DC: Political Research Associates, National Gay and Lesbian Task Force Policy Institute, and Equal Partners in Faith.

Knight, R., et al. (2004, January 7). *Marriage: One man, one woman.* Washington, DC: Family Research Council.

Kosciw, J., and Cullen, M. (2001). *The GLSEN 2001 national school climate survey: The school-related experiences of our nation's lesbian, gay, bisexual and transgender youth.* New York: Gay, Lesbian and Straight Education Network.

Kosovsky Sedgwick, E. (1990). *Epistemology of the closet.* Berkeley: University of California Press.

LaRue, J. (2004, January 27). Why *Goodridge* is legally and constitutionally wrong. Concerned Women for America Legal Studies.

Levin, D. (1997). The Constitution as rhetorical symbol in western anti-gay rights initiatives: The case of Idaho. In Witt, S., and McCorkle, S. (eds.). *Anti-gay rights: Assessing voter initiatives.* Westport, CT: Praeger. pp. 33–49.

Liu, G. (1999). Social Security and the treatment of marriage; spousal benefits, earnings sharing and the challenge of reform. *Wisconsin Law Review*. 1. pp. 1–64.

Logue, Patricia M. (2001). *The rights of lesbian and gay parents and their children*. New York: Lambda Legal Defense and Education Fund. www.lambdalegal.org/binary-data/LAMBDA_PDF/pdf/115.pdf.

Madison, J. (1987). Federalist 10. *The Federalist Papers*. New York: Penguin Classics.

Massachusetts Family Institute (2003, spring). *Issue in focus: Marriage affirmation and protection amendment*. Newton, MA: Author.

Mills, R., and Bhandari, S. (2003, September). *Health insurance coverage in the United States: 2002*. Washington, DC: U.S. Census Bureau.

National Center for Lesbian Rights (2002, September). *Legal recognition of LGBT families*. www.nclrights.org/publications/lgbtfamilies.htm#12.

Patterson, C. J. (1995). *Lesbian and gay parenting: A resource for psychologists*. Washington, D.C.: American Psychological Association. www.apa.org/pi/parent.html

People for the American Way Foundation (2002). *Hostile climate: Report on anti-gay activity*. 8th edition. Washington, DC: Author.

Peplau, L., and Spalding, L. (2003). The close relationships of lesbians, gay men, and bisexuals. In Garnets, L., and Kimmel, D. *Psychological perspectives on lesbian, gay, and bisexual experiences*. 2nd edition. New York: Columbia University Press. pp. 449–474.

Perrin, E. C., and the Committee on Psychosocial Aspects of Child and Family Health (2002). Technical report: Co-parent or second-parent adoption by same-sex parents. *Pediatrics*. 109(2). pp. 341–344.

Prager, D. (2004, March 2). San Francisco and Islamists: Fighting the same enemy. Posted on the Massachusetts Family Institute website under the heading "Timely Commentary." www.mafamily.org/commentary.htm.

Quinn, T. (2001). AIDS in Africa: A retrospective. *Bulletin of the World Health Organization*. 79(12). pp. 1156–1167.

Rayside, D. (2002). Recognizing same-sex relationships: Profiling change in Canada and the United States. Paper delivered at the annual meeting of the American Political Science Association, August 29–September 1, 2002, Boston, MA.

Regan, M. (2001). *Preserving marriage in an age of counterfeits: How "civil unions" devalue the real thing*. Washington, DC: Family Research Council.

Rennison, C., and Welchans, S. (2000, May). *Special report: Intimate partner violence.* Washington, DC: U.S. Department of Justice, Office of Justice Programs, Bureau of Justice Statistics. Revised January 31, 2002.

Renzetti, C., and Miley, C. (eds.) (1996). *Violence in gay and lesbian domestic partnerships.* Binghamton, NY: Harrington Park Press.

Republican National Committee (2000). *Platform 2000: Renewing America's purpose together.* www.rnc.org/gopinfo/platform.

Rust, P. (2001.) Two many and not enough: The meanings of bisexual identities. *Journal of Bisexuality.* 31. pp. 57–65.

Shaw, S. (1997). No longer a sleeping giant: The reawakening of religious conservatives in American politics. In Witt, S., and McCorkle, S. (eds.). *Anti-gay rights: Assessing voter initiatives.* Westport, CT: Praeger. pp. 7–16.

Sherrill, K. (2004). *Same-sex marriage, civil unions, and the 2004 presidential election.* New York: Policy Institute of the National Gay and Lesbian Task Force.

Shippy, R. A., Cantor, M. H., and Brennan, M. (2001, November). Patterns of support for lesbians and gays as they age. In M. H. Cantor (chair). *Social Support Networks.* Symposium held at the 54th Annual Scientific Meeting of the Gerontological Society of America. Chicago, IL.

Siculus, D. (1992). *Volume 11, Fragments of books 21–32.* Library of History (Loeb Classical Library). Cambridge, MA: Harvard University Press.

Simmons, T., and O'Connell, M. (2003). *Married-couple and unmarried-partner households: 2000.* Washington, DC: U.S. Census Bureau. www.census.gov/prod/2003pubs/censr-5.pdf.

Sprigg, P. (2003). Question and answer: What's wrong with letting same-sex couples "marry"? *Family Research Council In Focus.* Issue No. 256.

Stacey, J. (2001, July 9). Family values forever: In the Marriage Movement, conservatives and centrists find a home together. *The Nation.*

Stacey, J., and Biblarz, T. (2001). (How) does the sexual orientation of the parent matter? *American Sociological Review.* 66(2). pp. 159–184.

Stanton, G. (n.d.). *How good is Goodridge? An analysis of Goodridge v. Department of Public Health.* Colorado Springs, CO: Focus on the Family.

Stevenson, M. R. (2000). Public policy, homosexuality and the sexual coercion of children. *Journal of Psychology & Human Sexuality.* 12(4). pp. 1–19.

Towery, J. (n.d.). *Protecting the civil rights and religious liberty of faith-based organizations: Why religious hiring rights must be preserved.* Washington, DC: White House Office of Faith-Based and Community Initiatives. www.whitehouse.gov/government/fbci/booklet. pdf.

Traditional Values Coalition (n.d.). *Do homosexuals really want the right to marry?* Anaheim, CA: Author. www.traditionalvalues.org.

Traditional Values Coalition (n.d.). *Judges: Our robed masters; A call to end judicial tyranny!* Anaheim, CA: Author. www.traditionalvalues.org.

U.S. Census Bureau (2001). *Profile of general demographic characteristics: 2000.* Washington, DC: Author. www.census.gov/Press-Release/www/2001/tables/dp_us_2000.pdf.

Vaid, U. (1995). *Virtual equality: The mainstreaming of gay and lesbian liberation.* New York: Anchor Books.

Index